7 $\frac{50}{1}$

D0122459

DATE DUE

GAYLORD			PRINTED IN U.S.A.

CRITICISM AS DIALOGUE

CRITICISM AS DIALOGUE

WALTER STEIN

CAMBRIDGE
AT THE UNIVERSITY PRESS
1969

Published by the Syndics of the Cambridge University Press
Bentley House, 200 Euston Road, London N.W.1
American Branch: 32 East 57th Street, New York N.Y.10022

Library of Congress Catalogue Card Number: 69-12929
Standard Book Number: 521 07439 8

Printed in Great Britain
at the University Printing House, Cambridge
(Brooke Crutchley, University Printer)

TO MY WIFE

CONTENTS

ERRATA

p.117, l.10: *for* ankes *read* ankles

p.147, l.23: *delete* of

p.156, l.2: *for* to desperate farce *read* desperate farce

p.157, l.3: *for* go on living *read* to go on living

ACKNOWLEDGMENTS

This volume is based on work over a considerable period, much of which first appeared in the publications acknowledged below. The essays centre upon a number of closely related themes, and seek to sustain a coherent approach to the underlying critical questions. The material has been extensively revised and expanded.

I should like to express my gratitude to Professor S. G. Raybould and to the University of Leeds for enabling me to accept the William Noble Fellowship at Liverpool, from 1965 to 1967. Similarly, I am very conscious of my debt to Professor Kenneth Muir and his colleagues at the Liverpool English Department for offering me such privileged facilities in connection with this book and some related studies on which I am still engaged.

I also much appreciate the various kinds of help received from Mr Brian Wicker, Dr Keith Sagar, Professor W. Walsh, Professor Kenneth Allott, Professor Roy Shaw, Mrs Inga-Stina Ewbank and Dr Eric John. And I should like to thank the staff of the Cambridge University Press, for stimulating and constructive responses to my MS. Of course, I alone must take responsibility for the book as it now stands.

It would hardly be practicable to list my more general intellectual debts, though many of these will be evident from references within the book. But I cannot miss this opportunity to declare my special indebtedness in literary matters to Professor L. C. Knights, to whom I owe all

Acknowledgments

that a pupil can owe an inspiring teacher. And, in a very different way, it seems appropriate to recall what I owe to Fr T. V. Whelan, who received me into the Christian community to which I belong, to the late W. Schenk and to Frances Brice, who had helped to show me its relevance, and to Fr Herbert McCabe and Dr R. A. Markus, who have helped me to grope my way among the challenges we are living through.

Acknowledgments are due to the editors and publishers of *Essays in Criticism*, *The Northern Miscellany of Literary Criticism*, *Life of the Spirit*, *The Dublin Review*, *New Blackfriars* and *Slant*. Chapter 3—based on a paper given to a Downside Group conference at Leicester, in April 1964—was also included in a symposium, *Theology in Modern Education*, edited by Laurence Bright, O.P. (Darton, Longman and Todd). I am also grateful to Chatto & Windus Ltd and Stanford University Press for permission to quote extracts from Raymond Williams's *Modern Tragedy* in Chapter 6.

W. S.

'What you don't understand is that it is possible to be an atheist, it is possible not to know if God exists or why He should, and yet to believe that man does not live in a state of nature but in history, and that history as we know it now began with Christ, it was founded by Him on the Gospels. Now what is history? Its beginning is that of the centuries of systematic work devoted to the solution of the enigma of death, so that death itself may eventually be overcome. This is why people write symphonies and why they discover mathematical infinity and electromagnetic waves. Now, you can't advance in this direction without a certain upsurge of spirit. You can't make such discoveries without spiritual equipment, and for this, everything necessary has been given us in the Gospels. What is it? Firstly, the love of one's neighbour—the supreme form of living energy. Once it fills the heart of man it has to overflow and spend itself. And secondly, the two concepts which are the main part of the make-up of modern man—without them he is inconceivable—the ideas of free personality and of life regarded as sacrifice...It was not until after the coming of Christ that time and man could breathe freely. It was not until after Him that men began to live in their posterity and ceased to die in ditches like dogs—instead they died, at home in history, at the height of the work they devoted to the conquest of death, being themselves dedicated to this aim.—Ouf! I'm sweating like a pig. I might as well be talking to a blank wall.'

'That's metaphysics, my dear fellow. It's forbidden me by my doctors, my stomach won't take it.'

– Doctor Zhivago

1

INTRODUCTION:
DOGMA AND LITERATURE

It seems late in the day, no doubt, to reverse the emphasis of Matthew Arnold's formula. The 'inevitable revolution befalling the religion in which we have been brought up' which *Literature and Dogma* sought to accommodate has passed into history for us. The revolution we are now living through is merely the secularism in which we have been brought up. Even the newest of 'new theologies' may thus seem nothing but a progression of emergency responses to a culture well acclimatized to assimilating theology to astrology, alchemy or classical myth. Conversely, literature is studied from every conceivable angle —historical context and evolution, formal and linguistic achievement, psychology, moral and political impact— but rarely with any seriousness as a living metaphysical dialogue. Even *The Bible as Literature*, always a somewhat equivocal enterprise, has lately been overtaken by much more radical paradoxes—from 'religionless Christianity' to 'the theology of the-death-of-God'. And even the most popular contemporary theologizing frequently comes across as indistinguishable from atheism.

Yet this is also the age of Objections, Soundings, and Gods We Want; and one in which the word 'dialogue' has been rendered almost unusable, though we cannot avoid its use, by rapid, multiple inflation. In theory at least, liberal humanists, Marxists, Protestants and Catholics are all in a highly self-critical and receptive mood. Dogmatism is out; even the dogmatic repudiation of dogma, perhaps?

This paradox of an apparently hardening detachment from religious tradition that is joined with a freshly sensitized openness to religious concern cannot be traced to any single, clearly identifiable cause, or set of causes. In any case, we are much too deeply immersed in this situation to see it steadily or whole. Long-term and short-term influences, beyond our powers of discrimination, continue to flow in upon our shifting fields of vision. The growing urge towards self-criticism within each sector of modern commitment—or non-commitment—is hardly distinguishable from pressures accumulating from the world as a whole. Can any of us be sure how far the present rapprochement between Marxists and Christians is due to the nuclear facts of contemporary coexistence, how far to the inner logic of Marxist and Christian concerns? Or how far is the drawing together of Christian bodies a direct (if belated) response to imperatives of reconciliation—and growing up—how far a closing of ranks in the face of secularist advances? Have atheists and agnostics succeeded in evolving philosophies, or patterns of sensibility, more essentially adequate to human intelligence and aspiration than the traditions they would displace? Are contemporary theological efforts to assimilate the secular ethos, and to re-create Christian concepts and Christian communities all along the line, an authentic renewal of Christian life, or a massive internal collapse, masked by pretentious double-thinking?

Dogma and Literature

No one who faces these questions in any depth will be tempted to simple, doctrinaire answers; that is the burden, and privilege, of our time. Each area of major enquiry or action insists on directing us back towards the critical problems it poses. In the end these problems are metaphysical. They confront us with metaphysical choices and inquests, whether we care for metaphysics or not, whether we acknowledge them as metaphysical or not. What sort of a being man is, in what sort of a world he has his being, what ultimate 'meanings', if any, human life has, are the classical metaphysical questions; and we are reaching the end of the era whose metaphysic of anti-metaphysics could carry the day without any acknowledged metaphysical thinking at all.

By and large—in principle, at least—this is now accepted even by academic philosophers in Britain. On the Continent, despite all the pressures of positivist ideology, there has never been a time when academic philosophy appeared to anathematize metaphysics—each and every possible form of metaphysics—*ex cathedra*. In Britain, however, A. J. Ayer's *Language, Truth and Logic*, of 1936, came extraordinarily close to such a performance on behalf of professional philosophers nurtured in the tradition of Bacon, Locke and Hume, as well as in the climate of contemporary scientific triumphalism. As it gradually sank in that this elegant, merciless declaration was itself essentially 'metaphysical' by its own criteria (since it could hardly be just a tautology, still less a scientific hypothesis —the only two forms of statement exempted from nonsensicality), logical positivism gave way to the *aggiornamento*—at once revolutionary and deeply traditional—of the later Wittgenstein.

But though linguistic analysis is, in principle, open to all the traditional human pursuits, not excluding metaphysical and theological pursuits, its impact in these areas has been rather restricted—a greater force *within* contemporary theology than as a meeting-ground of modern minds as a whole. This may partly be due to the fact that many of its leading British practitioners continued, as persons, to operate with sensibilities not in fact so very remote from Ayer's after all; it may also be bound up with the 'logical' (rather than phenomenological) emphasis of its analytic techniques, and their relative remoteness from every-day culture—the contrast, here, with French existentialism, for instance, is obvious and telling.

So it is that literary, rather than philosophical, investigations carry the major burden of metaphysical consciousness in modern Britain: if literature has always, by nature, tended towards metaphysics, the sparseness of formal metaphysical thinking in our time cannot help placing a special responsibility upon the metaphysical functions of literature. One might have expected, therefore, that literary criticism would reflect this situation by a correspondingly central stress upon these functions. The fact is, however, that academic literary studies, whilst recognizing that literature cannot be dissociated from 'the history of ideas', largely continue to shy away from any such direct metaphysical engagement.

In this sense, modern criticism still falls within the Matthew Arnold era; just as recent 'secular theology' is often remarkably foreshadowed by the Arnold of *Literature and Dogma*. It is Arnold—rather than Coleridge —who remains active in modern critical emphases on 'attitudes' and 'maturity', on 'pseudo-statements'— rather than 'vision'. His religious strengths (like his insistence that God is 'a term *thrown out*, so to speak, at a not fully grasped object'—not a 'fixed and rigid' idea) as well as his complacent, wholesale surrender of dogmatic tradition and metaphysical concepts point directly to present ferments. The distance between Arnold's reduction of religion to 'morality touched by emotion' and contemporary 'religionless Christianity' is no greater in its own sphere than that between the essentially 'emotive' theory of poetry emergent in Arnold's criticism and the reductive psychologism that (for all his debts to Coleridge) was to be formulated by I. A. Richards. Arnold's aloof dismissal of Christian doctrine, almost as if metaphysical seriousness were a species of philistinism, foreshadows both the anti-metaphysical secularism of our own time and its theological counterparts, striving to keep up with the secularists. Similarly, his concern to rescue 'poetry' from 'fact' opens the way to I. A. Richards's resolute theorizing, which bifurcates language in such a way as to leave literature relating to nothing but 'our interests, desires, feelings, attitudes, tendencies to action and what not'; so that literary ideas become essentially 'fictions', poetry is radically divorced from knowledge—and the notion 'that an objectless belief is a ridiculous or an incomplete thing' appears as 'a prejudice deriving only from confusion'.

Dogma and Literature

The parallel between Arnold's reduction of religion to 'morality touched by emotion' and of poetry to 'idea'—'idea' in dissociation from 'fact'—is of course much more than merely a parallel; it springs from a single cultural root, and defines a single cultural strategy:

The future of poetry is immense, because in poetry, where it is worthy of its high destinies, our race, as time goes on, will find an ever surer and surer stay. There is not a creed which is not shaken, not an accredited dogma which is not shown to be questionable, not a received tradition which does not threaten to dissolve. Our religion has materialised itself in the fact, in the supposed fact; it has attached its emotion to the fact, and now the fact is failing it. But for poetry the idea is everything; the rest is a world of illusion, of divine illusion. Poetry attaches its emotion to the idea; the idea *is* the fact. The strongest part of our religion to-day is its unconscious poetry.

Thus—quoting himself—Arnold opens his essay on 'The Study of Poetry', of 1880. We need only refer to this reiterated conception of the poetic to feel the pulse of Arnold's religiosity. The power of poetry is, here, ultimately a power of immunity to 'the fact'; as the religion of *Literature and Dogma* is ultimately a retreat into a 'poetry' seen in these terms. In T. S. Eliot's concise diagnosis, the aim of Arnold's religious writings was 'to affirm that the emotions of Christianity can and must be preserved without the belief'. And the 'high destinies' of poetry, as Arnold conceived these, lay in providing 'an ever surer and surer stay' amidst the threatening Future of an Illusion (the Freudian *reductio* was itself almost around the corner): a new, and surer, 'illusion' in fact.

In the essay on Arnold and Pater just referred to, Eliot goes on to suggest that from Arnold's proposition 'two different types of man can extract two different types of conclusion: (1) that Religion is Morals, (2) that Religion is Art. The effect of Arnold's religious campaign is to divorce Religion from thought'. Arnold himself pioneered the first route, Pater the second. It would not be difficult to trace their progeny to the present day; sometimes the line of descent converges from both. But a third group of consequences, now even more dominant, might be expressed by reversing these conclusions, namely: (3) Morals/Art is Religion—ideological absolutes, or art as a pseudo-religious cult. Where art begins to see itself as transcendently self-sufficient—from Yeats's equivocal play, in *Sailing to Byzantium*, with his 'artifice of eternity', or Joyce's declared ambition, in the *Portrait*, to 'transmute the daily bread of experience into the radiant body of everlasting life', to Mr Peter Brook's up-to-date offerings of ritual for ritual's sake in the theatre—art, irrespective of content, turns into a kind of opium of the intellectuals. And at the same time we have been, and remain, subject to the paralysing disorientations—'The best lack all conviction'—of Yeats's *The Second Coming* and the complementary 'passionate intensity'—'The ceremony of innocence is drowned'—of our century's ideological blood-offerings. The wheel has come full circle. Even idolatry is a kind of religion.

Yet it is of the nature of post-religious religiosity to 'fall apart'; again and again (if necessary), through its own contradictions, it must 'wither into the truth'. Hitler and Stalin survive in us as warning signals; revolutionary nostalgias have lost their innocence. Conversely, the residual 'Christian civilization' that sustains established injustices, and fails to incarnate—to give real presence to—the hope beyond all hopes which it represents, is virtually reduced to the condition it should redeem. And so a Christianity displaced from its own deepest identity and a secular humanism that is heir to parodic second comings of messianic passion, confront each other across recent traumas with renewed potentials of learning and growth; as both together confront those (cheerful or cheerless) cutters of losses whose tamed, doctrinaire disillusion would cut human potentiality down below size. Even those religious institutions which continued, well into the present century, to defend their strenuous orthodoxy by sheer, resolute exclusions of modern awareness, have at last begun to open themselves, in full seriousness, to the adventure of radical dialogue.

The essays in this volume are offered as a contribution towards this dialogue. As such, they address themselves to two main sets of questions: concerning the place of literature in human self-orientation; and concerning specific aspects of this orientation.

Of course these questions often converge. Two of the following chapters, however, 'Christianity and the Common Pursuit' and 'Criticism as Dialogue', centre directly upon the cognitive status of literature and literary studies, and their relevance to metaphysical and theological concerns. The former reviews modern English criticism, and especially the work of F. R. Leavis, in relation to the problem of literature and belief, and enquires into the pertinence of specifically Christian contributions to modern criticism. The latter examines the importance of literary studies to Christian believers themselves—and specifically for contemporary theological education. Thus their emphases are essentially complementary, and I hope that they will be seen in this way.

At the same time, these chapters begin to explore areas within which the common pursuit of human self-orientation—including, but going beyond, what is usually meant by critical 'judgment'—takes place. We may demarcate three such areas: (i) the quest for personal and social fulfilment; (ii) tragedy and frustration; and (iii) the quest for transcendent meanings. It is within these interacting fields of human awareness and response that the adequacy, or inadequacy, to reality of any given imaginative structure emerges.

'Adequacy' is hardly a clear and distinct idea; indeed, it is almost as elusive as 'reality' itself (and we should remember Eddington's well-known caution: 'Reality! Loud cheers!'). Yet we cannot really do without either of these terms; and only a totally inadequate, Cheshire Cat, view of imaginative activity could simply withdraw into I. A. Richards-type 'objectless beliefs' as the proper object of literary experience. The question is not whether 'adequacy to reality' is pertinent to our encounters with literature, but what these words verbalize or imply, what forms, and degrees, of 'adequacy' we have to reckon with, what criteria, or procedures of assessment of what is 'real', we should bring into play.

A full theoretical answer to these questions would involve a massive philosophical operation on several fronts —including logical, epistemological and meta-critical analyses; and though such an undertaking is overdue— nothing approaching the stature of R. G. Collingwood's *Principles of Art* (1938) has emerged amidst recent developments—I obviously cannot pretend to attempt this. My own approach to these questions is, I hope, sufficiently indicated by these opening chapters. In any case, this approach depends upon the interaction of specific critical perspectives; it is through the practical confrontation of such perspectives that any orientation must emerge.

In this context, then, 'adequacy to reality' is a matter of concrete critical enquiry; though it also implies some kind of global, synthetic activity of orientation. I am afraid that phrases like 'synthetic activity of orientation' are apt to contract modern stomachs even more alarmingly than the word 'reality' itself. And with good reason. For not only are they rather a mouthful; but we have, after all, had our fill of metaphysical syntheses, grandly irrelevant to our shifting, multiplying, evolving, menaced, irreducibly fragmentary existence. Syntheses are what petrified into the 'heap of broken images' of *The Waste Land*; or what, in *Waiting for Godot*, came to think Lucky's shattered automatic thoughts. It's useless pretending we are where we aren't. We just cannot go back to all that.

Indeed, we cannot. But nor, I take it, can we be content to sit finally immobile, like Estragon and Vladimir, saying 'let's go', or entertaining even the most mature, complex objectless beliefs, with trained critical judgment, amidst the fallen and falling towers. After all, the author of the *Waste Land* is also the author of *Four Quartets*. Whatever, 'touched by emotion', underlies these two poems, they can hardly be both *equally* decisive, or decisive in the same sense—even for theories of morality touched by emotion, or for emotion attached to the idea (not the fact), or for emotional maturity, fineness of sensibility, civilized values, creative exploration, or cultural health. In the end we have to choose. Or, if simple choice is impossible, we at any rate have to assimilate the relevant continuities or breaks ('only connect!'). Even Beckett's in both senses synthetic Lucky has, at the core of his deep scholastic, scientific, literary and democratic fossilization a real centre of living awareness—a consciousness precisely of life-imprisonment among the fossils, a heart beating to the finality of 'labours unfinished', 'reasons unknown', and 'the great cold alas alas in the year of their Lord six hundred and something'. What bearings has the play in which he figures upon the *Waste Land*, *or* upon *Four Quartets*, *or* upon the spiritual logic that validates, or fails to validate, their sequence? And what bearings have all these works upon other 'visions of reality'—our tragic inheritance from Shakespeare; or Lawrence's reassertion of personal plenitudes; or Brecht's scalding imperatives of social hope? 'Things fall apart'; but we—each of us, and the communities that have shaped us—are either mere flying, centrifugal debris (or that which the debris is burying), or active centres of dialectical confrontation and commitment.

Dogma and Literature

To be engaged in such a confrontation, to be led towards such a commitment—a commitment that finds adequate room for (that does not disown, or shut out, or degrade) what it cannot judge fully 'adequate' in itself—*is* a synthesizing activity; the whole impetus of such activity is towards some sort of total orientation. But this activity need not aspire to any sort of static, invulnerable system. If the only alternatives were an exploding spiritual multiplicity and newly petrifying ideological rivalries, there really would be no escape from that 'shape with lion body and the head of a man' rousing us to the knowledge

> That twenty centuries of stony sleep
> Were vexed to nightmare by a rocking cradle,
> And what rough beast, its hour come round at last,
> Slouches towards Bethlehem to be born?

Since Yeats wrote *The Second Coming*, his beast has begun to take on the most extraordinarily concrete outlines: Stalinism, Hiroshima, Vietnam—even that other Final Solution—are only shadows of the nightmare capacities now at hand. If anything can arrest its slouch, it will be a common stock-taking, sufficiently awake, and sufficiently radical, to reach out towards new responses to old questions—and towards new insights into old answers. The notion of adequacy to reality, however problematic, and however demoralized by the centuries, is a notion we cannot afford to throw to the beast.

To assess whether, or in what degree or respects, a given approach to reality is 'adequate' to it need not, fortunately, imply a renewed hardening of metaphysical awareness. Indeed, metaphysical adequacy can now be seen

precisely as a kind of cumulative relation to experience—
an open-ended responsiveness to human growth. In art,
as in life (as in science), the most basic tests relate to experienced immediacies—which may, however, be subject
to exacting specific disciplines. This adequacy, in literature, includes not only immediate descriptive precision
and evocative power, but emotional proportionality
and modes of cultural focusing. These latter take us to
the well-established problems of creative realization,
stylistic influences, stock-responses and sentimentality.
Further, as soon as we come to grips with works of any
considerable background of reference, emotional or intellectual, an additional set of problems arises. Has anything essential been excluded from attention? Has anything
invalid been included in the total picture? Here we confront the varieties of literary evasion. This of course is
rarely a conscious, or fully conscious, manœuvre.
'Adequacy' now becomes a matter of the degree of
authentic reflection—of the creative surmounting of
occasions of evasiveness. (These are especially prominent
in the field of tragedy, but also wherever any kind of
emotional need, or intellectual presupposition, is active
within the field of vision.) Finally, and most problematic
of all, there is the challenge of works—from *King Lear*
or *The Winter's Tale* to *Women in Love* or *Four Quartets*—
whose nature is to offer some sort of total image of, and
orientation towards, essential human experience. Nor need
this kind of challenge be confined to works of this scope;
it can present itself in miniature in quite short poems—*The
Windhover*, for instance, or *Among School Children*. It is

at this level, of quality and reach, that the notion of 'adequacy' presses against its precarious ultimate limits. In an obvious sense its retention here verges on mere impertinence; in another sense, however, it is among creations of this authority that a proper seriousness towards what confronts us *exacts* their mutual confrontation as images of existence, a weighing of their ultimate 'adequacy to reality'. In the end, criticism thus tends towards a metaphysical dialectic. And, far from this being an impertinent intrusion into critical tasks, criticism can stop short of such metaphysical lengths only at the cost of an ultimate shrinking back from the authorities it confronts:

> The rhetorician would deceive his neighbours,
> The sentimentalist himself; while art
> Is but a vision of reality.

If Yeats is right here, then even the greatest achievements of art—the greatest, indeed, above all—require us to look into their 'adequacy', precisely as claimants to an ultimate orientating authority.

The three dimensions of 'adequacy' just indicated may conveniently be referred to as (a) adequacy of expression, (b) adequacy of exposure, or encounter; and (c) adequacy of total orientation. Criticism has always regarded itself as a proper judge of (a)—'expression' in the Croce/Collingwood sense—and has also ventured into judgments of (b), as a sort of deeper extension of (a). Clearly these two types of adequacy often cannot be separated in practice, though (a) is the more basic—always presupposed by (b). In its turn, (c) of course presupposes (a) and (*b*), being a further, ultimate depth within them. Here, however, critical assessment becomes so patently, centrally metaphysical (and problematic) that the tendency is either to pull up sharply before this point (but my case is that this is, in effect, to shrink from an adequate confrontation) or to rush in with *a priori* metaphysical maps where critical explorers fear to tread. A proper dialectical criticism must start from an equal acceptance of its metaphysical tasks and their inescapably problematic demands; it must reach out, through the most adequate confrontation and self-exposure it can achieve, towards the visions of reality that confront it.

But if what is being demanded here is as problematic as this, are we not heading for simple impossibilities—or, still worse, for a ravenous dogmatism in explorer's clothes? We can only hope to show that such demands need not be self-defeating by an actual critical search, or series of searches. And this is what most of the essays in this volume seek to do. It might be possible to formulate principles descriptive of, or normative for, such critical confrontations; but not only would this be an immensely complex and delicate task, it would anyway be a secondary kind of task, as grammar and logic are secondary to the emergent thrust of living language. The character, and viability, of a criticism committed to dialectical confrontations, in a search for an orientating 'adequacy', can only show itself in actual critical practice.

From this point of view, it is less important that readers should assent to the 'findings' of these essays than that they should feel satisfied that a criticism of this kind is capable of handling problems of ultimate belief in appropriate, disciplined ways. I hope that these essays will at any rate help to show that critical activity need not stop short of a total activity of orientation, in order to hold off alien, totalitarian interests: that the interests of literature and the interests of metaphysical dialogue, far from necessarily conflicting, may essentially coincide.

Since my concern is especially with present encounters between secular humanism and Christianity, there is a special emphasis on modern writing. And since this encounter seems to me to have its most crucial location in the area of the tragic, the emphasis further falls on tragic literature and tragic theory. It is here, amidst the facts of tragedy and frustration (especially, of course, the fact of death) that fundamental attitudes towards personal and social fulfilment, on the one hand, and towards religious transcendence on the other, are brought to the test.

The juxtaposition of Lawrence and Beckett in Chapter 3 leads into areas—overlapping and interacting—within which secular aspirations and tragic experience act out their complex, multiple tensions. Chapter 4 seeks to pursue these problems to a point where we can begin to assess the 'adequacy' of secular and Christian responses to tragic facts. Focusing upon the relations between *King Lear* and the drama of Chekhov, it attempts to diagnose the pressures that have led to contemporary displacements of traditional tragic forms by the peculiar fusions of tone now dominant both in the theatre and in modern culture generally. This chapter is pivotal for the whole discussion. I hope it will be evident how each of the three levels, or dimensions, of 'adequacy' which we have noted enters into the picture, and especially how various kinds of pressure towards 'evasion'—which criticism is competent to diagnose—can limit or erode the adequacy even of such deeply powerful visions as Chekhov's. Conversely, the absolutely inexhaustible poise of *Lear*—relentlessly, insupportably assaulted from within, yet firmly inviolate and inviolable in orientation—offers a totally actualized norm of 'adequacy to reality'.

One can hardly overstress the obvious fact that mere proximity of a writer's apparent affiliations to one's own cannot be evidence of such 'adequacy'. And of course this holds equally whatever one's beliefs, though the pitfalls will vary in complementary ways. Yet, just as obviously, if 'belief' is indeed a crucial factor in the relations between writer and reader, it would be disablingly false to suppose that such proximities should be somehow bypassed or played down. I hope that Chapter 5, which centres on some of T. S. Eliot's specifically Christian writing, indicates how a Christian critic may seek to combine a proper acknowledgment of his own beliefs with a proper alertness to Christian pitfalls.

This chapter also develops the more general examination of the currents shaping awareness of human potentialities and limits, sacred and secular claims, in our time. Eliot's voice is, above all, absolute for death. His tragic recognitions never desert him. His problem is precisely that of evoking a 'glory' that does not write off the world it would redeem—the world of experienced fruition and heartbreak—for a transcendence totally beyond worldly facts. It is here, in Eliot's tendency to insulate sacred meanings from life's inherent potentialities within time, that his authority is apt to dwindle, that he is most in need of Lawrentian—and Brechtian—correctives.

Thus there are important aspects of Eliot's vision (and not only in his earlier work) that border directly on Samuel Beckett's—the vision most directly converse to Lawrence's—though there are crucial potencies in Eliot as unavailable to Lawrence as to Beckett. For Lawrence's *Rainbow* bridge between the finite world and 'infinity', superbly incarnate as it is, yet lacks a dimension that a fully poised image like *Lear* or *The Winter's Tale* possesses —and which Eliot, whatever his limitations, possesses too: a proportionate sense of tragedy.

There is every reason to think that Lawrence's turning away from full tragic exposure springs from an active, central refusal—directly related to the direction of his achieved growth. His early work indicates a sensibility potentially fully open to the tragic; from *The White Peacock*, with its last sentence, 'He sat apart and obscure among us, like a condemned man', to a great deal in *Sons and Lovers* and—most remarkably of all—the vision of *The Widowing of Mrs Holroyd*. But soon his writing, both critical and creative, acquires a potent resistance to tragic ultimacies. The beginnings of this process are already hinted at in *Sons and Lovers* when Paul Morel—'at the core a nothingness, and yet not nothing'—decisively shuts his fists:

'Mother!' he whispered—'mother!'
She was the only thing that held him up, himself, amid

all this. And she was gone, intermingled herself. He wanted her to touch him, have him alongside with her.

But no, he would not give in. Turning sharply, he walked towards the city's gold phosphorescence. His fists were shut, his mouth set fast. He would not take that direction, to the darkness, to follow her. He walked towards the faintly humming, glowing town, quickly.

Henceforth in Lawrence's work there are episodes of loss or defeat, characters that destroy or are destroyed, the vision of a destructive civilization; but the essential Lawrentian stance is to refuse to 'give in'—if necessary even at the cost of 'turning sharply' from the facts, from whatever threatens to tempt towards 'the darkness'. He will no longer admit tragedy into the centre of his awareness. If tragic realities press in upon his world, they must at any rate be kept subordinate: whether by further developments within a time sequence; or by simple refusals of imaginative sympathy; or—as with the contrasted couples in *Women in Love*—through holding a negative, diagnostic structure firmly in place by a more centrally weighted counter-structure of fulfilment (or at least potential fulfilment).

In view of what Lawrence achieved within these limits —and, for all we know, in virtue of these limits—one could hardly wish his achievement other than it is. Even more plainly, though in converse respects, Samuel Beckett's limitations are intrinsic to his importance. There is nothing at all unusual about such complementary powers and limits. Indeed, we must expect that, outside a very small circle of centrally normative images of existence—total in scope, and totally proportionate to this scope (I'm thinking again especially of Shakespeare's tragedies and last plays)—even the greatest writers' visions are in need of continual counterbalancing. Yet when one considers T. S. Eliot's case, the tendencies that thus limit his work do not seem to be thus intrinsic to his achievements; they are, so to speak, incidental to his growth, and indeed in essential opposition to its demands. We may identify them as, on the one hand, a tendency to write off the created world, as if the Waste Land were incapable of being made truly fertile by the Incarnation; and on the other hand—closely bound up with this—a certain withdrawal from tragic directnesses towards the end of his career. Thus we have the extraordinary fact that Lawrence and Eliot are most in conflict where, by Eliot's own deepest commitments, they ought most to converge: in the quest for meanings in human relations; and that, at the same time, they should arrive, by opposite routes and means, at a major negative agreement: their practical tendency away from tragedy. In Lawrence this tendency is entirely of a piece with his most deeply valuable affirmations, though it limits, and sometimes vitiates, them. In Eliot's case, however, it is at first sight almost unintelligibly paradoxical. That a poet so essentially rooted in tragic authenticity should end his career with a series of near-tragedies, teased into farcical moralities for the West End, is the sort of critical shock that sets off far-reaching reorientations all around the scene. It is sure to tell us as much about the Christian/humanist culture-gap and about unresolved contradictions within contemporary Christianity itself as about Eliot's personal

career. Is the post-Christian sensibility of its nature in-
hospitable to tragic directnesses? Is Christianity itself
finally incompatible with tragedy? Is tragic art—or, at
least, are traditional forms of tragic art—an anachronism?

These questions, and questions related to them, are reviewed in the concluding essay, 'Humanism and Tragic
Redemption'. Taking the form of a dialogue with Raymond Williams's *Modern Tragedy*, this essay seeks to
gather the implications of the preceding discussions into
a framework of tragic theory. In doing so, it pursues the
enquiry more explicitly into its social and political
bearings, and brings liberal hopes and despairs, Marxist
social redemption and Christian transcendent meanings
into confrontation. One would hardly expect any simple,
handily packaged answers from such an enquiry—and I
hope that such pitfalls have been avoided, equally with
the alternative temptation, to a vacuous, evasive hotch-
potch. A discussion like this should reckon with a complex
of loosely emerging problems and pointers, surrounding
a centre of orientation sufficiently formed to facilitate
further searches—and meetings with other centres.

It seems to me that Raymond Williams's revolutionary
humanism, as developed in *Modern Tragedy*, picks up a
number of central challenges in the life and letters of our
time that will enforce themselves with increasing urgency
during the era that is now emerging. Unlike the *Scrutiny*
generation of critics, to whom Raymond Williams's work
is indebted, Williams is as directly concerned with
political action as with academic literary studies (even
in the dedicated, wide sense that *Scrutiny* gave to these

studies). But also, unlike so many who have sought to bring modern literary and political concerns into active relation, he really has the interests and equipment of a serious literary critic. *Modern Tragedy* bears the fruits of this conjunction; though its special significance, both literary and political, seems to have been almost entirely missed on its appearance. The diagnostic light that the book throws—from its special angle—upon the relations between Lawrence and Eliot, Camus, Sartre and Brecht, needs to be reckoned with, whatever one's own conclusions. Then, behind this, there is a theoretical reconsideration of the whole notion of 'tragedy'—and of how tragic awareness might develop within contemporary culture—that similarly requires one's response in depth. And, at the other pole, the notion of 'revolution' is subjected to a critique for which 'tragedy', thus redefined, is crucial—enforcing attention to moral dilemmas habitually by-passed from opposite directions. It is a genuinely reciprocal process of literary and political redefinition. This is where its essential challenge lies.

All this does not imply that Williams's work may not be open to serious objections and qualifications. Indeed, my own response to its claims includes many emphatic 'Yes, buts', both on a technical plane, and regarding its substance. Mostly, these are all bound up with limitations intrinsic (it seems to me) to Williams's chosen fulcrum. By this I do not mean that where he succeeds he succeeds *in spite of* this fulcrum or centre of orientation: his importance is essentially bound up with this stance—and his analytic definition of its implications; but so, equally, are the question-marks that might need to be placed against his findings. Williams's modified Marxism—a Marxism seeking an authentic, humane response to man's tragic situation—cannot authentically be brushed aside with ready-made liberal or Christian objections. To the extent that one is prepared to take the weight of its emphases, it should at any rate be impossible to disown the pressures upon one. Equally, however, it seems to me that Williams's Marxist redefinitions do not suffice, in the end, to break through towards an 'adequate' responsiveness to human experience. Too much that is essential in life and art continues to be left out or displaced from the centre of reorientation that emerges.

Pointing to what seems to me still 'inadequate' in the humanism of *Modern Tragedy*, my concluding chapter seeks at the same time to give firmer definition to my own standpoint: that of a radical Christian humanism. If the conjunction of these three words should ring like paradox piled on paradox to some readers, I hope that they will at any rate accept this description provisionally. Of course, the word 'humanism' is often used to denote an atheist or agnostic view of the world, so that it might at best seem a form of semantic confusion, at worst a double-thinking mystification (as I myself would regard the current theological fashion of 'Christian atheism') to speak of a 'Christian humanism'. Actually, however, any difficulty here itself springs from a confusion of meanings. Of course if anyone wishes, in appropriate contexts, to use the term 'humanism' as a purely negative counter—relative to theistic beliefs, he is free to do so, though I think that this is almost a *technical* use, however widely this use is now in currency. That there is, however, nothing inherently normative in such a use of the word is evident both from its history and from its still irrepressible positive implications. Thus, the word's active connections with 'the humanities' (and, in a special way, with classical studies) point back to the literary culture of the renaissance Humanists. Its rich positive force, as we commonly use it today, is partly derived from these roots, partly from the associated idea that 'humanism' (as the O.E.D.'s second definition has it) is simply 'the quality of being human; devotion to human interests'.[1] This, surely, is the central strand of meaning implied whenever the word acts as more than a counter-theological pointer. And, obviously, there can be no valid *a priori* necessity to reserve 'the quality of being human; devotion to human interests' to systems of thought or action 'concerned with *merely* human interests (as distinguished from divine), or with those of the human race in general (as distinguished from individual); the Religion of Humanity' (the O.E.D.'s third definition; italics added). Indeed, we need only think of Erasmus and Thomas More to remind ourselves how intimately 'the quality of being human; devotion to human interests' (for surely this sense is strongly present, in addition to the classicist sense, when we recollect their humanism) may be joined with Christian beliefs.

[1] The first definition reads: 'Belief in the mere humanity of Christ. 1812'. But this is now a relatively rare use, whilst the word 'humanist' appears as early as 1589 in its classicist sense; though, as attached to 'humanism', the O.E.D. lists this last—as sense 4.

If, therefore, one wishes to speak of 'humanism' or 'humanists' in senses necessarily precluding theistic commitments, one will either have to rely on the context to make this clear, or will need to add adjectives like 'atheistic', 'agnostic' or 'secular'—or to substitute some such term as 'secularism'. Clearly, the ambiguities of the word 'humanism' are not merely a fact of language; they embody an inevitable conceptual plasticity within a pluralist culture. After all, we are all human. Nevertheless, the term is not vacuous: being human does not necessarily ensure 'devotion to human interests'; and there are resonances in the term, irrespective of its associated adjectives, that circumscribe 'the quality of being human' it postulates. These resonances are well caught, I think, in Jacques Maritain's opening pages of *True Humanism* (whose concern is precisely to analyse the bases of Christian humanism):

We shall at least be on our guard against defining humanism by exclusion of all reference to the superhuman and by a denial of all transcendence. Leaving all these points of discussion open, let us say that humanism (and such a definition can itself be developed along very divergent lines) essentially tends to render man more truly human and to make his original greatness manifest by causing him to participate in all that can enrich him in nature and in history...It at once demands that man make use of all the potentialities he holds within him, his creative powers and the life of the reason, and labour to make the powers of the physical world the instruments of his freedom.

What exactly will 'tend to render man more truly human' will of course depend on our conception of what man is. But the notion of human 'greatness', and of man's creative relation to the physical world, is already latent in this normative emphasis—whether an essential reference to transcendent meanings is also to be included or not.

Thus, Christianity is of its essence a humanist religion. The Old Testament doctrine of the Creation ('And God saw that it was good'; 'And whatsoever Adam called every living creature, that was the name thereof') is already profoundly humanist. The doctrine of the Incarnation ('And the Word was made flesh, and dwelt among us') renders this humanism, literally, divine. In a sense, therefore, the phrase 'Christian humanism' is tautologous: Christianity cannot be other than humanist in virtue of its most central doctrine.

That it is nevertheless necessary to affirm Christianity's 'humanism' is only partly due to the semantic muddles we have noted; there is an even more urgent necessity to affirm it in view of the fact that Christian culture has so often failed to perceive—or act out—that this is what the Incarnation implies. For a variety of complex historical reasons—sociological, philosophic, temperamental, moral—Christian tradition, Catholic as well as Protestant, has again and again failed to meet its humanist commitments. This is its essential historical failure, both in relation to itself and in relation to 'the world'.

In this failure, misleading interpretations or emphases with regard to three of its other doctrines have played a decisive role. Partly as consequence, partly as cause, these doctrines have been seized on in ways that obscure the full meaning of the Incarnation. Thus the Fall and the Crucifixion have been closely associated with a virtual writing off of human potentialities within time. And a purely apologetic exploitation of the Resurrection (as a 'proof' of Christ's divinity) completed this dislocation of Christian centralities—dissociating the tragic imagery of man's fallenness and Christ's cross from divinely human powers of rising, and helping to raise—the 'new creation' inaugurated by Christ's Resurrection, into which man is called to be reborn.

Thus, to stand within a '*radical* Christian humanism' is to seek a more effective understanding of man's vocation in history and a more effective embodiment of the Christian vocation within this vocation. It is to open oneself equally to time's tragic inheritances and to the incipient wonder of their redemption. It is to seek to 'redeem the time'—not to flee from time; yet still to recognize that 'we have here no abiding city'—that the fullness of human rebirth cannot be the transformation of temporal experience alone.

The eschatological absolutes of the Second Coming are thus to be felt not as an alternative to real historical values, creativeness and hopes, but as their transcendent consummation and *raison d'être*. The Kingdom that is not of this world is, nevertheless, a Kingdom for the world's sake—and already incipient within the world. The story of the rabbi who, in face of the announcement of the Messiah, looks through the window and says 'I see no change', could be a radical Christian parable.

Over against the emphases of conventional otherworldliness (very often a licence for an only too thorough accommodation with the world) a radical Christian humanism believes that the world must, and can, be 'changed'. Against individualist piety, it affirms the communal bonds of personal existence. Against clerical institutionalism it places the claims of human needs of which the Christian presence should be the leaven. If the sacraments are empowered symbols which 'bring about what they signify', the 'real presence' of Christ in the Eucharist is essentially a revolutionary presence: demanding that the Kingdom come—and be seen to be coming: a daily bread of deliverance from evil.

Yet this sacramental optimism remains a tragic optimism. Its faith in human potentialities does not disown human limits and cosmic estrangements. Its distinctive reunifying resources are sacrificial. Its distinctive ultimate hope points to a transcendent, cosmic atonement.

In his Introduction to Roger Garaudy's *From Anathema to Dialogue* (1967), Karl Rahner, the great Jesuit theologian of the *aggiornamento*, suggests that man's real essence might actually be defined as 'the possibility of attaining the absolute future'; and that 'the absolute future is merely another name for what is really meant by "God"':

What Christians call grace is nothing other than God's self-communication as the absolute future in that stage in which the history of its accession and acceptance is still continuing.

In these terms, we could say that a radical Christian humanism sees its task as the active, transforming reception of the incipient absolute future. This does not at all imply that the future is predictable: only that history is a meaningful process—subject to divinely significant ends; so that (despite all empirical errors, disasters and deformations) it is divinely grounded in hope. It does not imply that human activity is capable of creating 'the absolute future': but, on the contrary, that 'the absolute future'—God's eschatological imminence 'face to face'—is already at work, as attraction, 'in a glass darkly', within the relativities of our historical strivings. It does not mean that the Kingdom of God is nothing but juster, more loving historical relations; but that such relations are imperative thrusts towards the Kingdom's ultimate, transfiguring reception as a gift—the end (in both senses) of history.

Such an outlook should have dynamic, synthesizing potentialities that need not succumb to ideological disorders. Of its essence, it is at once personalist and societal, feminine and masculine, accepting and revolutionary. It affirms, absolutely, the reality and values of time, whilst looking beyond temporal limits for their real, ultimate meaning and fulfilment. It knows real tragedy, as the arena of our fallen condition; but also as the ground of resurrecting sacrifice; and perceives, with the eye of faith, that, even at 'the extreme verge' of the most absolute 'cliffs of fall' (more than anywhere, perhaps, at this verge) the absolute future is incipient.

The tendency of these essays, then, is to suggest that a radical Christian humanism is the most adequate—the only really adequate—orientation available to us; and that this 'adequacy' is open to dialectical enquiry. Which is not to say that other orientations can be dismissed, or even that they can be assumed to be anything less than essential within the common pursuit of human commitment. Neither life nor literature is a knock-out tournament. At the same time, though, we do live *one* life; to which all literature is related:

> Though leaves are many, the root is one...

And this is not merely an abstract metaphysical reflection. It is a direct postulate of maturing experience. Yeats's four-line poem is, after all, called *The Coming of Wisdom with Time*:

> Though leaves are many, the root is one;
> Through all the lying days of my youth
> I swayed my leaves and flowers in the sun;
> Now I may wither into the truth.

Kierkegaard once protested that, whilst philosophy is full of problems, life is full of choices. But thought itself may demand vital commitment; and life itself is a rough and ready dialectic.

Whether in life, art or thought, the two endemic temptations of our age are withering forms of commitment—or non-commitment. So habituated are we to these alternatives, and so conscious of the special dangers of ideological fever or sclerosis that 'chronic open-mindedness' has almost come to appear like a mark of health. But, though there are commitments that kill, there are commitments that give life. Christians must certainly be constantly on the watch against allowing their faith to turn into ideology. But this is itself a part of their real commitment (they do not carry the absolute future around in their pockets); and, if they are faithful to it,

Dogma and Literature

they will, in truly essential ways, remain creatively open to experience. And such a commitment should at any rate ensure a serious metaphysical *availability*: a true readiness to confront ultimate questions. For their part, secular humanists might perhaps be prepared to consider whether their own approach may not sometimes give rise to a simple by-passing or shrugging off of questions one 'doesn't believe one has answers to'—and hence to academicism and triviality?

A dialectical criticism merely acknowledges that there is a real essential connection between the leaves and the root, between the coming of wisdom and truth. How 'wisely' can the leaves and the flowers be 'judged' without pronouncing upon the root, hidden from the dance in the sun? (Could the dancer and the dance, however resistant to separation in thought, be enacting anything but a fusion of lies if their only viable dialectic were a withered, and withering, emergence into reality?) The rhetorician would deceive his neighbours, the sentimentalist himself, but the serious reader or critic can ultimately respond to the leaves and flowers before him only as visions going to the root.

2

CHRISTIANITY AND THE
COMMON PURSUIT

What is Christian criticism? Is there, in fact, such a thing as a specifically Christian contribution towards this activity?

It certainly cannot be taken for granted that there is. Physics, say, history, and literary criticism are three distinct activities, and each again distinct from metaphysics and theology. Is there, then, a Christian physics? a Christian history? a Christian criticism? The whole immense range of problems of the relations between sacred and secular, autonomy and integration, seems to open out before us.

There is, of course, no blanket solution to these problems. Physics is not in the least like history or criticism, and radically different relations obtain, according to the basic character of each activity. We neither can, nor need, attempt to trace a comprehensive framework of disciplines and the kind of autonomy or interpenetration that should rule among them. It is sufficient to remind ourselves of this wider perspective within which our problem has its setting; for its solution will depend partly upon the general structure of the Christian humanist ideal (with its recognition, in principle, of various kinds, or degrees, of autonomy in various spheres of action and thought), partly upon the internal logic of the critical function itself.

It is from this latter side that our problem must

necessarily be approached. Once the principle of autonomy, or at least subsidiary autonomy, in various fields
has been set down (we might think of Newman's sort
of formulation, or Maritain's) the precise position of each
discipline must be left to define itself mainly through that
discipline's own practice—and reflection upon that
practice.

What, then, is criticism, and what are its peculiar
methods?

We may take as our starting-point a passage from
Robert Graves's *Goodbye to All That*, prefixed to F. R.
Leavis's *The Common Pursuit*.[1]

At the end of my first term's work I attended the usual
college board to give an account of myself. The spokesman
coughed and said a little stiffly: 'I understand, Mr Graves,
that the essays that you write for your English tutor are, shall
we say, a trifle temperamental. It appears, indeed, that you
prefer some authors to others.'

That is as good a working definition of criticism as
we are likely to come across: to prefer some authors to
others, to the scandal, or the amusement, of one's tutor.
And, in a sense, we may never get very far beyond it.
For it may be suggested that, while any genuine critical
judgment is necessarily objective in reference (which, of
course, does not preclude fallibility), it is always peculiarly
'personal' in form. Such a judgment emerges from the
critic's innermost grasp of, and response to, the work in
its complex uniqueness; so that it will be informed by
his antecedently organized responses to life, and at the

[1] London, 1952

3 33 SCA

same time be found irreducible to any terms other than itself. To put it another way, literary judgments presuppose a variety of 'standards'; but these standards, if they are vital, are always embodied—uniquely embodied —in particular critical acts, not applied from the outside, like a ruler or a rule. They have, indeed, no full existence outside their embodiment in this or that act of valuation.

In that sense, then, the critical judgment simply is what it is, and nothing remains to be added. Further discussion, however, may arise under any of the following three headings. Granted that a literary judgment is 'personal', unique, and irreducible, while at the same time it is objective in reference: what, in the first place, disciplines or controls it? Secondly, what is such a judgment's content: whence is it derived and what, ultimately, validates it? And what, thirdly, are its relations to other types of judgment, especially those of morality, metaphysics and theology? These divisions, though not arbitrary, are far from watertight; the three groups of questions flow into each other, and are ultimately inseparable.

I

To the first of these problems, as to the disciplining of literary judgments, a complete and (it appears to me) completely satisfying solution is provided in the work of F. R. Leavis. It is this problem with which he has always been most centrally concerned: the very word 'discipline', in the context of literary studies, immediately calls up his name. Throughout his writings, there is a persistent, jealous stress upon the specific 'business of the critic'; which is, or ought to be, 'a discipline of thought that is at the same time a discipline in scrupulous sensitiveness of response to delicate organizations of feeling, sensation and imagery'.[1] Thought and sensitiveness—'intelligence and sensibility together'[2]—that is how the emphasis should fall. And no doubt, in theory, this is universally accepted. It is, of course, only through its actual exercise in particular tasks of perception, analysis and judgment that the discipline can be given true definition.

Dr Leavis is at great pains to distinguish this irreducible function of 'the intelligence and sensibility together' from the neighbouring activities of the sociologist, philosopher, or theologian; who, he insists—unless they also possess, and scrupulously bring into play, that 'disciplined relevance in response, comment, and determination of significance'[3] which makes the critic—will be led into the most blatant impertinences when it comes to judging works of literature. 'Literary criticism', he writes (the occasion is an exchange with the philosophically-minded American scholar, René Wellek)—

Literary criticism and philosophy seem to be quite distinct and different kinds of discipline—at least I think they ought to be (for while in my innocence I hope that philosophic writing commonly represents a serious discipline, I am quite sure that literary-critical writing commonly doesn't). This is not to say that a literary critic might not, as such, be the better for a philosophic training, but if he were, the advantage, I

[1] *Education and the University*, London, 1943, p. 38.
[2] *Ibid.*, p. 34.
[3] *Scrutiny*, vol. XV, no. 2 (Spring 1948), p. 99.

believe, would manifest itself partly in a surer realization that literary criticism is not philosophy...The business of the literary critic is to attain a peculiar completeness of response and to observe a peculiarly strict relevance in developing his response into commentary; he must be on his guard against abstracting improperly from what is in front of him and against any premature or irrelevant generalizing—of it or from it. His first concern is to enter into the possession of the given poem (let us say) in its concrete fulness, and his constant concern is never to lose his completeness of the possession, but rather to increase it. In making value-judgments (and judgments as to significance), implicitly or explicitly, he does so out of that completeness of possession and with that fulness of response. He doesn't ask, 'How does this accord with these specifications of goodness in poetry?'; he aims to make fully conscious and articulate the immediate sense of value that 'places' the poem.[1]

This stress on 'relevance' in 'developing response into commentary', on 'completeness of possession and... fulness of response' is untiringly reiterated throughout Dr Leavis's career, and given its full weight in the course of his actual critical practice and inspired hints like the following:

The critic will be especially wary how he uses extraneous knowledge about the writer's intentions. Intentions are nothing in art except as realized, and the tests of realization will remain what they were. They are applied in the operation of the critic's sensibility...These tests may very well reveal that the deep animating intention (if that is the right word) is something very different from the intention the author would declare.[2]

[1] *The Common Pursuit*, pp. 212–14.
[2] *Scrutiny*, vol. xv, no. 2 (Spring 1948), p. 99.

We need only to bring to mind *Brighton Rock*, say, or *The Cocktail Party*: where, surely, we have a fair conception of their authors' willed artistic purpose; but find that, on closer inspection, both these works are much more radically—disablingly—'negative' in their 'deep animating intentions' than their authors 'would declare'. It is this kind of context, perhaps, which presents the greatest temptations to the Christian to do violence to his critical integrity. It certainly has to be confessed that, again and again, Dr Leavis has been able to enforce charges against Christians (as well as Marxists) of 'debasing the currency and abrogating the function' of criticism, by permitting doctrinal or apologetic concerns to usurp a sphere in which the critic's disciplined sensibility should preside.

II

The first duty, then, of the Christian in criticism is to be indeed nothing less than a critic. I have put the point as forcibly as I could, by allowing Dr Leavis to make it for me.

We now have to pass on to the second and third groups of questions confronting us: relating to the essential *contents* of literary judgments—whence they are derived, and what, ultimately, validates them; and the problem of their *relations to other types of judgment*, such as those of a moral, metaphysical, or theological kind. I think that these two groups of problems are best approached together.

At this point we can no longer simply rely upon

Dr Leavis's guidance; but it may be useful to formulate our qualifications with continued reference to his position so as to define, as sharply as we can, the frontiers that we have in common.

In his urgent preoccupation with 'intelligence and sensibility *together*'[1] (as the marks of a specifically 'critical' discipline), Dr Leavis may have been led into an undue disregard for conceptual thought as such, including the conceptual presuppositions of his own critical practice. It is one thing to write, as T. S. Eliot does, in his early Preface to *The Sacred Wood*, that 'when we are considering poetry we must consider it primarily as poetry and not another thing'; or, as Dr Leavis himself puts it, that 'the moral judgment that concerns us as critics must be at the same time a delicately relevant response of sensibility': it is another thing to conclude that 'abstract' moral (or metaphysical) norms have no relevance, or that the critic, as critic, need not engage in the sort of inquisition that is directed towards *the conceptual analysis of his own judgments*. 'The critic', we read,

The critic...is indeed concerned with evaluation, but to figure him as measuring with a norm which he brings up to the object and applies from the outside is to misrepresent the process. The critic's aim is, first, to realize as sensitively and completely as possible this or that which claims his attention; and a certain valuing is implicit in the realizing. As he matures in experience of the new thing he asks, explicitly and implicitly: 'Where does this come? How does it stand in relation to...? How relatively important does it seem?' And the organization into which it settles as a constituent in becoming

[1] My italics.

'placed' is an organization of similarly 'placed' things, things that have found their bearings with regard to one another, and not a theoretical system or a system determined by abstract considerations.[1]

Is this really the whole of what takes place in a literary valuation? We have already agreed with Dr Leavis in the rejection of the idea of any kind of norms which the critic 'brings up to the object and applies from the outside'. But does it follow that a literary judgment is through and through a function of 'things' finding their bearings with regard to one another internally—and nothing else? Do those 'abstract considerations'—moral, philosophic, or theological—with which the critic comes to his poem or novel play no determining part at all in his judgment? In literature, as elsewhere, everything is what it is and not another thing; and it is right and necessary to recognize this. But, equally, in literature as elsewhere, everything has its own degree, or kind, of independence in the scale of human activities and not some other. Is it not evident that, although literary valuations should always, in part, be an emergent function of literary experience itself, their ultimate content must necessarily be derived from the critic's apprehension of life in its entirety—including the conceptual frameworks he has come to accept? And that therefore a literary judgment transcends the 'discipline' in terms of which it is exercised?

There are many places where Dr Leavis seems to recognize this with full force. 'The more seriously one is concerned for literary criticism', he writes, 'the less

[1] *The Common Pursuit*, p. 213

possible does one find it to be concerned with that alone.'[1]
Or, more explicitly still, he speaks of there being 'hardly
any need to illustrate the ways in which judgments of
literary value involve extra-literary choices and decisions'.[2]
Why, then, does he so often write as if the judging were
self-sufficient? And why does he so resolutely refuse to
accord to those 'extra-literary choices and decisions' a
basic acknowledged place in the critical function itself?
What, for instance, are the extra-literary choices and
decisions that impinge upon Dr Leavis's fine advocacy of
Four Quartets? After all, whatever the distinction between
a fully realized poetic utterance and a doctrinal 'frame',
we have here a poem which not only is, as he indicates,
'a searching of experience, a spiritual discipline, a technique for sincerity—for giving "sincerity" a meaning',[3]
but a poem whose essential significance cannot be
separated from such lines as:

These are only hints and guesses,
Hints followed by guesses; and the rest
Is prayer, observance, discipline, thought and action.
The hint half guessed, the gift half understood is Incarnation.
Here the impossible union
Of spheres of existence is actual...

—and in which there occurs the phrase:

The poetry does not matter.

We know, of course, that the poetry matters very much
indeed, and that it is T. S. Eliot himself who has said:

[1] *For Continuity*, Cambridge, 1933, p. 160.
[2] *Ibid.*, p. 183.
[3] *Education and the University*, p. 89

'When we are considering poetry we must consider it primarily as poetry and not another thing', but it seems evident that Dr Leavis's response to the work either tends to stop short the nearer it moves towards its centre, or in fact takes him farther in the way of extra-literary commitments than he is prepared to follow through. He is well aware that lines like those just referred to 'are, no doubt, statements, to be taken as such'; and we fully subscribe when he continues:

but though they imply a theological context, their actual context is the poem. It would be absurd to contend that the passage is not an invitation to a relating of the two contexts, but nothing is gained from the point of view of either poetry or religion by an abandonment of one context for the other, or by an approach that refuses or ignores or relaxes the peculiar discipline that the poetry is.[1]

We can accept all this (we are back to our initial point, in fact) and agree that the Christian reader may easily be tempted towards a kind of short cut—a too easy 'jumping in with familiar terms and concepts' that might lead him to miss the specific, complex fullness of the poem, its distinctive exploratory achievement. But when it comes to appreciating not merely the poet's 'genius' and *the quality of the level at which his exploration is conducted*, but to a final estimate of *the nature and validity of his findings*, is it irrelevant what sort of 'abstract considerations' the critic may bring to his reading—or be invited to take away with him from it? If, as Dr Leavis says, 'it would be absurd to contend that the passage is not an invitation to a

[1] *Ibid.*, pp. 102–3.

relating of the two contexts'—the poetic and the theological—and 'nothing is gained from the point of view
of either poetry or religion by an abandonment of one
context for another', surely it is as vital not to 'abandon'
the theological truth arrived at (for it is truth or it is
nothing) for the poetic discipline in which it is embodied,
as it is not to 'abandon' that discipline for the doctrinal
framework in which, nevertheless, it finds its completion.
We cannot read great literature without being carried
beyond it. We cannot, in the last resort, judge it, without
being judged in our own fundamental convictions.

III

What, then, is the position of the critic who is a Christian?
If the foregoing account is correct, then he must clearly
be a *Christian critic*—that is, the fact that he is a Christian
should enter intimately into the kind of criticism he produces; while at the same time he will constantly be subject
to the demands of the critical discipline as such.

If Christian criticism has often, in practice, failed to win
the respect of other critics, this is not because there is an
'orthodoxy' behind it (though, unfortunately, that is the
impression the non-Christian will often carry away) but
simply because the critic has failed as a critic. There is
nothing in the least inevitable about this kind of failure.
And the cure for it is surely a greater awareness of the
critical function; not a suppression of the critic's most
deep-seated springs of judgment when he comes to his
work as a critic.

Christianity and the Common Pursuit

In many respects the ideal Christian critic would be indistinguishable from the ideal liberal one. For not only would they share a common conception of their task, but over a wide area of experience their specific responses and valuations would be likely to coincide. 'Liberalism' at its best—Matthew Arnold's kind of liberalism rather than Jeremy Bentham's—remains predominantly a secularized form of Christian humanism (and, incidentally, not at all comfortable with its agnostic burden). Whether or not such a humanism, in dissociation from Christian doctrine, seems to us logically tenable, or whether or not we believe that it stands any chance of survival, is beside the immediate point. Here and now liberal humanism remains a force; and a unity of implicit valuations, if not at the level of ultimate acceptances, can still be elicited in many contexts among liberal and Christian traditionalists. In a world engulfed in ever-increasing intellectual bewilderment (and there are senses in which the Christian cannot escape the fullest participation in this plight) one of the most urgent practical tasks is to strengthen, and re-define, our common commitments, at the level of actual specific valuations, towards the tradition in which we stand.

It is not any diversion, or narrowing, of critical sympathies (relative to the liberal's) that ought to distinguish the Christian critic's contribution but, on the contrary, its openness to an extra dimension. Obviously, for instance, he should be qualified to enter the universe of *Four Quartets* with a completeness denied to the secular critic. But should he not also—though this will seem a much more dubious claim—be equally at an advantage

43

in the confrontation of works that, in various ways, fall outside any 'orthodox' framework? Great care is needed here to avoid misunderstanding. The critic, if he is doing his job, cannot operate from the outside, with the help of a series of theological norms: if he does not sit down humbly in front of his poem or novel, prepared to receive it first of all on its own terms, and allow his response to develop from the centre of his personality, he will have nothing relevant to contribute. Just as it is not sufficient that a work should be 'Christian' in overt intention to commend it at the level of embodied sensibility, a 'non-Christian'—even, perhaps, an 'anti-Christian'—work may be charged with vital insights at the 'natural' level and even with religious aspirations of which it is itself unaware. As D. H. Lawrence emphasizes, in a well-known passage—a favourite of Dr Leavis's:

It is the way our sympathy flows and recoils that really determines our lives. And here lies the importance of the novel, properly handled. It can inform and lead into new places the flow of our sympathetic consciousness, and it can lead our sympathy away in recoil from things gone dead. Therefore the novel, properly handled, can reveal the most secret places of life—for it is in the *passional* secret places of life, above all, that the tide of sensitive awareness needs to ebb and flow, cleansing and refreshing.[1]

It is at this level—of the ebbing and flowing of 'sensitive awareness', of 'the most secret places of life'—that a piece of literature really has its being; and there is no short cut to what it is. It cannot be measured by its formal

[1] Quoted in *For Continuity*, p. 120.

credentials. What it 'is', moreover, may not offer itself to any simple acceptance or rejection; more often than not we have to delimit and qualify and check and re-check the ways in which we expose ourselves to its influence, or in which we confront it with our resistance. All this is part of the ordinary business of critical reading, and wherever we do less we disqualify ourselves as judges. Nevertheless, every kind of criticism finally depends upon 'extra-literary choices and decisions' of one sort or another, and it is claimed that a Christian humanist perspective offers a combination of rootedness and openness which should serve it well in 'the common pursuit', if only it is adequately represented by its exponents.

IV

Acknowledging, then, that 'extra-literary' norms and principles of judgment must again and again rediscover themselves newly reflected in the stream of particulars, and that adequacy at that level is a *sine qua non* of the critical function, Christian criticism may submit a three-fold claim to an advantageous perspective in the task of arriving at ultimate evaluations.

1. From its own point of view, these are all derived from the first: the faith that Christianity is the standpoint of truth. Here and nowhere else, of course, is the real motive of a specifically Christian approach to art; and it is here—beyond the limits of critical technicalities—that the ultimate credentials of Christian criticism are to be found. This only needs insisting upon since so many

of our contemporaries regard dogmatic Christianity as not merely on the defensive in the contemporary intellectual climate, but as no longer standing in any relevant relationship towards it. 'Criticism', writes one of its distinguished present practitioners,

Criticism, more than most intellectual activities, seems to me conditioned by the current relationship between words and thought. This relationship is determined by the dominant social trends of the moment, and today these are *not* specifically Christian. If a contemporary critic is to be vocal he has necessarily to be non-Christian.[1]

Christianity is heavily under pressure, to be sure. But can it really be assumed that criticism, in any given situation, must conform passively to 'the dominant social trends of the moment'; that it does not, on the contrary, assert a direct, active relationship to *truth*; which transcends any merely 'dominant' trends, bearing to these only a secondary, incidental kind of relation? And if it be agreed, first, that such a direct relation to truth is indeed intended in critical judgments and, secondly, that the content of these judgments must always be very largely 'extra-literary', then the Christian claim to a serious hearing can hardly be avoided.

2. But while it is the intrinsic truth of Christianity which the Christian himself would affirm as the essential source and validation of Christian criticism, non-Christians may perhaps recognize that such a perspective —whatever its extra-literary claims—might have some

[1] F. W. Bateson, in a private letter; I very much appreciate Mr Bateson's consent to my present use of this statement.

real *critical* advantages. And the second of our claims is that Christianity does indeed offer a perspective of judgment privileged in its combination of rooted unity, openness and metaphysical reach.

(i) Christian criticism derives its unity and direction from the intellectual and cultural tradition of which it is a product; just as liberal criticism must be *eclectic*, precisely to the extent to which it is removed from this central inheritance. Liberal criticism *must* be eclectic: since it can only be defined in terms of negations, hesitancies and qualifications relative to the Christian civilization from which it springs. This eclecticism is accordingly present, in various forms and degrees, in the majority of modern critical writings. It is above all this lack of unified direction which, for instance, limits the ultimate achievements of William Empson's analytic brilliance: nobody knows better how to throw an exciting hard light upon half a dozen lines of poetry or the Structure of a Complex Word, but he never seems to have attained to any consistency of analytic tact or a corresponding purposive centrality of judgment.

(ii) But unity and purposiveness do not by themselves guarantee a valid critical procedure. Indeed, as we have already noted, these qualities carry with them very considerable dangers—the pitfalls pointed to by Dr Leavis in his campaign against critical 'orthodoxies', both Marxist and Christian. We shall do well to remember, for example, John Strachey's delightful and celebrated vision of *Ash Wednesday* as a product of the capitalist boom of the 'Twenties—

Since writing *The Waste Land* Mr Eliot, encouraged no doubt by the 1922–1929 period of capitalist recovery, has left the despair of *The Waste Land* behind him and taken up the typical position of a highly intellectual reactionary,[1]

or Philip Henderson's view of Marlowe's *Faustus* as

simply a parable of the fight for intellectual freedom, and the conflict set up in his mind between this desire and his mediaeval heritage of fear and superstition, which, in its turn, was simply a reflex of political and economic subjection that the Church has always consecrated and ordained by God.[2]

(Accordingly, we learn, 'Superstition enters in the shape of the Good Angel' whilst Faustus's 'progressive and adventurous impulses appear externalized in the shape of the Evil Angel'; and the hero, at the end, is unfortunately 'hauled off to hell before he can realize any of his dreams' since 'technical knowledge was still far too elementary for any of these prospects'.)[3] It is well to attend to such instances of 'purposive' criticism not because Marxist discussions of literature are always on this sort of level, or because Christian critics never fall into crudities of their own, but precisely as danger signals relevant to Christian practice. And a further important point calls for notice. There is plenty of Christian criticism that is deficient; and there is some impressive criticism by Marxists. But the deficiencies of Christian criticism, it may be suggested, are always accidental: they reflect deficiencies in individual sensibility. With Marxist criticism, however, the opposite

[1] Quoted by L. C. Knights, in *Drama and Society in the Age of Jonson*, London, 1937, p. 2.
[2] *And Morning in His Eyes*, London, 1937, p. 310.
[3] *Ibid.*, pp. 312–17.

would seem to hold: it is the narrower interpretations and judgments which emerge most faithfully out of a Marxist perspective. For whilst Marxist categories can diagnose some essential aspects of art and history as nothing else can, it is only a section of human experience that can properly be approached in this way; and wherever a more comprehensive response is required, Marxist critics either cease to be adequate critics, or to be genuinely Marxist in their response. Writers like Edmund Wilson, Christopher Caudwell and Arnold Kettle, all of whom have produced criticism worthy of respect, would furnish instances of both kinds of reaction to this dilemma.

For the Christian humanist, however, such a dilemma does not arise. If he fails in his work as a critic the responsibility is wholly and specifically his own. For, unlike the Marxist's, his intellectual perspective should endow him not only with a purposive unity of vision but also with infinitely varied and comprehensive potentialities of response. Because of his doctrinal commitments his vision will always be framed within 'orthodoxy'. But because this orthodoxy centres upon the doctrine of the Incarnation—the reality of both spirit and flesh, their opposition and their oneness, their degradation and divine renewal; because it is both personalist and societal; and because—in proportion to the authenticity of its *faith*—it is itself intimately exposed to the pressures of unbelief: this framework is for ever open to fresh disclosures of experience—at once traditionalist and revolutionary, permanently engaged on assimilating the shocks and pressures and exaltations of the unceasing flux of change.

(iii) Christian criticism, then, should enjoy special advantages in virtue of its unity, its openness and, lastly, its metaphysical reach.

It is free of the metaphysical inhibitions which the liberal often cultivates as marks of intellectual honour, and it avoids the liberal tendency to pull up short of 'discovery', the emphasis being fixed on 'exploration'.

We may illustrate the liberal's characteristic self-arrest first of all with reference to one of its most extreme manifestations, I. A. Richards's theory of meaning. The theory is sufficiently well known to absolve me from having to restate it in any detail. What may be suggested is that one of the principal motives behind its construction —the radical division of language and mental processes into 'referential' (i.e. cognitive) and 'emotive' (quite divorced from any cognition)—was Dr Richards's desire to defend the importance of imaginative writing, without having to confront its metaphysical challenges. Literature, he concedes, often *looks* as if it touched upon problems of truth; but in fact it only involves '*emotional* belief'— which has no cognitive significance whatever. 'Its only justification is its success in meeting our needs—due regard being paid to the relative claims of our many needs one against another.'[1]

Now, if Dr Richards were a philistine busy-body, dabbling beyond the limits of his true gifts, this astonishing theory could simply be passed over. But of course this is by no means the case: again and again he will come out with the most perceptive and illuminating suggestions,

[1] *Practical Criticism*, London, 1929, p. 277.

nourished by authentic first-hand encounters with literary experience; it is only in some of his moods as a theorist, and especially as an amateur liquidator of metaphysics, that he ceases to command respect. And even there, his theory at least has the merit of bringing into the open the liberal's predicament as a critic.

Take, for instance, his remarks concerning tragic *catharsis*:

It is essential to recognize that in the full tragic experience there is no suppression. The mind does not shy away from anything, it does not protect itself with any illusion, it stands uncomforted, unintimidated, alone and self-reliant. The test of its success is whether it can face what is before it and respond to it without any of the innumerable subterfuges by which it ordinarily dodges the full development of experience. Suppressions and sublimations alike are devices by which we endeavour to avoid issues which might bewilder us. The essence of Tragedy is that it forces us to live for a moment without them.[1]

We may have our reservations about this (we might question that phrase 'alone and self-reliant', for example), but so far as it goes, it is a valuable contribution towards the analysis of tragic experience. So far as it goes. For the natural slant of our minds irresistibly urges us to further questions—questions no longer psychological, but irreducibly metaphysical in reference. What, we want to ask, is the reality that *enables* us to face the utmost terrors of experience without illusions and suppressions and yet emerge with that 'sense of release, of repose in the midst of stress, of balance and composure'[2] which tragedy gives?

[1] *Principles of Literary Criticism*, p. 246.   [2] *Ibid.*

What have we *seen* through our 'pity and terror'? It is here that Dr Richards suddenly lets us down. The passage quoted above continues:

When we succeed we find, as usual, that there is no difficulty: the difficulty came from the suppressions and sublimations. The joy which is so strangely the heart of the experience is not an indication that 'all's right with the world' or that 'somewhere, somehow, there is Justice'; it is an indication that all is right here and now in the nervous system.

Lear, then, is good for our nervous system, that is all we know on earth and all we need to know. But what if we should feel compelled to enquire further?

Well, we could hardly do better than return to Dr Leavis. His essay on 'Tragedy and the Medium' is a fair example of the quality of his work; and, as it happens, it contains some incidental criticisms of Richards's passage on tragedy not far removed in tendency from the observations just made. Leavis's own formulation specifically dissociates his analysis from any such self-centred emphasis, and at the same time pushes the whole problem beyond a merely psychological level. Notice how he progresses from delicate psychological observation towards something far beyond the limits of subjectivity:

The sense of heightened life that goes with the tragic experience is conditioned by a transcending of the ego—an escape from all attitudes of self-assertion. 'Escape', perhaps, is not altogether a good word, since it might suggest something negative and irresponsible...Actually the experience is constructive or creative, and involves a recognizing positive value as in some way defined and vindicated by death. It is as if we were challenged at the profoundest level with the question,

52

'In what does the significance of life reside?', and found ourselves contemplating, for answer, a view of life, and of the
things giving it value, that makes the valued appear unquestionably more important than the valuer, so that significance lies, clearly and inescapably, in the willing adhesion
of the individual self to something other than itself.[1]

Dr Leavis then goes on to cite passages from Derek
Traversi and D. W. Harding further developing these
hints, and then concludes, before addressing himself towards a rather different aspect of the problem:

I will not attempt to develop the kind of discussion of Tragedy
that the juxtaposition of these passages might seem to promise
—or threaten. It suits my purpose rather...[2]

And off he turns to his new point. Now this final refusal
to 'develop the kind of discussion of Tragedy' that he
might have seemed to promise (and that ambiguously
deprecating 'or threaten') is as characteristic of Dr Leavis's
work as the masterly precision and authority of what he
does allow to emerge before pulling himself up short. A
critic expressly Christian in allegiance might perhaps
have felt freer to threaten—or promise?—to develop that
kind of analysis after all.

3. This brings us to the last of the considerations that
Christian criticism might advance in defence of its own
validity. We have discussed, first, its extra-literary assumption of standing in the perspective of truth; secondly, the
critical advantages consequent upon this outlook: its
unity, its openness, its metaphysical reach; and now,
finally, we may consider whether the very finest of our

[1] *The Common Pursuit*, pp. 131–2.   [2] *Ibid.*, p. 133.

'liberal' critics do not in fact fail to be 'Christian' only in a kind of ultimate refusal to take the full measure of the assumptions and implications of their own practices.

Dr Leavis would be pretty certain to repudiate, with fully alarmed vigour, any attempt to celebrate his work as not only the classical moment of twentieth century criticism but, more specifically, as classical in the line of *Christian* discrimination. And yet, is it a mere eccentric impertinence to regard him in some such way? Consider, for instance, his remarks on tragedy just quoted. It led us to observe that a critic with Christian commitments might have taken that kind of analysis still further. But perhaps not so very much further after all: that is how we must now circumscribe our suggestion. For, whatever his reticences, Dr Leavis hardly leaves us in any doubt as to the reality towards which tragic experience would seem to point. He explicitly repudiates what he calls 'Senecan' types of interpretations—interpretations in which tragic *catharsis* corresponds to some sort of ego-centric uplift ('the mind stands uncomforted, unintimidated, alone and self-reliant', says Dr Richards); leaving, as the only possible kind of alternative—well, what?

It is as if we were challenged at the profoundest level with the question, 'In what does the significance of life reside?', and found ourselves contemplating, for answer, a view of life, and of the things giving it value, that makes the valued appear unquestionably more important than the valuer, so that significance lies, clearly and inescapably, in the willing adhesion of the individual self to something other than itself.

Would a professedly Christian critic necessarily wish—or feel able—to penetrate so very much further in explicit

Christianity and the Common Pursuit

analytic comment? Would Dr Leavis's kind of comment be intelligible, or be capable in the end of intellectual assimilation, outside an actively religious (if not specifically Christian) framework of acceptances? And is it, after all, so very far removed in tendency from, for instance, John F. Danby's[1] and R. B. Heilman's[2] (independently formulated) suggestion that the unsurpassed horror of *King Lear* generates what is essentially a *Christian* acceptance, and even joy, in the spectator?

This discussion of tragedy is not an isolated case. Again and again Dr Leavis assists us towards kinds of insight whose necessary implications can find sanction only within the fullness of religion. And he does so not only when confronting such specifically Christian challenges as the poetry of Hopkins or the later Eliot; but also relative to such contexts as the novels of D. H. Lawrence and E. M. Forster.

Is it merely an accident that the most important critics now writing (similar tendencies can, for instance, be traced in some of the work of L. C. Knights)[3] should so often approximate to a practically Christian stance? Or that among specifically Christian critics, some of the best, such as Derek Traversi and Martin Turnell, clearly owe important debts to *Scrutiny* and its founder? Is it not

[1] *Shakespeare's Doctrine of Nature*, London, 1944.
[2] *This Great Stage: Image and Structure in 'King Lear'*, Louisiana State University Press, 1948.
[3] E.g. in his magnificent essays on '*Macbeth*' and 'George Herbert' (the latter especially interesting in this connection, in view of its announced intention 'to define the human, as distinct from the specifically Christian, value of his work'); *Explorations*, London, 1946, pp. 1–39 and 112–130.

rather that the special distinction of the 'Leavisite' approach is ultimately even more a matter of its vitally active traditionalism at the level of judgment than of its brilliant analytic demonstrations, in terms of which these judgments are enforced? The question is whether such a traditionalism is autonomous; whether—logically, or historically—it can sustain itself merely by its own impetus.

Dr Leavis has always insisted that 'we still have a positive cultural tradition', that it is the business of criticism (as of education) to 'preserve and develop a continuity of consciousness and a mature directing sense of value—a sense of value informed by traditional wisdom'. And to this recognition, and Dr Leavis's untiring efforts, as critic and teacher, to substantiate and diffuse it, we owe so much that it may seem unfitting, almost a kind of betrayal, to suggest that, fine as it is, such advocacy of 'tradition' cannot, at this juncture, finally avoid an explicit inquisition into its sanctions. But, though the kind of liberalism Dr Leavis represents is a historical fact—and a fact the Christian can only rejoice in—it is difficult to believe in the possibility of its survival, unless it can replant itself in the religious sanctions it has left behind.

Dr Leavis might reply, in terms that he used in his *Education and the University*:

I assume that the attempt to establish a real liberal education in this country—to restore in relation to the modern world the idea of a liberal education—is worth making because, in spite of all our talk about disintegration and decay, and in spite of what we feel with so much excuse in our many despondent moments, we still have a positive cultural tradition. Its persistence is such that we can, in attempting at an ancient university an experiment in liberal education, count on a sufficient measure of agreement, overt and implicit, about essential values to make it unnecessary to discuss ultimate sanctions, or provide a philosophy, before starting work. This I assume; and I believe further that what is unnecessary is best avoided. That is, the kind of effort I have in mind would be the effort of an actual living tradition to bring itself to a focus, and would see itself—or feel itself—in terms of the carrying-on of a going concern. It may be said that here I am offering theory and doctrine; their drift, then, is that we should deal as much as possible in the concrete, the actual and the particular, and not expend ourselves overmuch on the definition or exploration of values and sanctions in the abstract.[1]

There is of course a great deal in this statement that compels assent; and my own argument approaches its position at many points. But, as Dr Leavis himself stresses, the passage, and its surrounding argument, relate specifically to conditions at an ancient university: very much less, we must add, to those prevailing at London, say, Manchester or Leeds; and in what relation does it stand to the 'dominant trends' of our civilization outside the walls of academic institutions? And even at the ancient universities themselves, how much longer can 'a going concern' be assumed, or a discussion of 'ultimate sanctions' be left in abeyance?

Finally, even if 'the preoccupation is not' (or, at any rate, not first and last) 'with the generalities of philosophical and moral theory and doctrine but with picking up a continuity',[2] still, we can only pick up something no longer firmly in our hands; and then, if we neither

[1] *Education and the University*, p. 18.
[2] *Ibid.*, p. 19.

accept the standards (or standardlessness) of the uprooted present, nor the complete (the 'orthodox', the traditionally sanctioned) body of implicit valuations, how can we avoid either an explicit defence of the principles by which we *select* among the various elements of 'tradition', or else a return to the fullness of 'orthodox' assents?

As D. S. Savage, has put it, in *The Withered Branch*:

Because the life of western man stands inescapably in a relationship to the Christian faith which has provided the foundations for his culture and civilization, so his art is, willy-nilly, positively or negatively, in a similar relationship. The disintegration...is that of a *Christian* culture; what meaning it has is, inevitably, a religious meaning.[1]

Logically this formulation is faulty: the disintegration of Christian culture could equally well have a purely secular meaning. Nevertheless, a real dilemma is posed. Either the meaning of this disintegration *is* religious in some sense; in which case we need to lay hold on this sense. Or it is indeed merely secular; in which case we must either shed our religious inheritances altogether, or learn to define precisely in what senses, in what contexts, and within what limits, these inheritances can remain 'a going concern' for us. The critic cannot, in the end, avoid committing himself upon this crux. In any case, it seems a final vindication of the idea of a Christian criticism that our greatest living critic, though specifically concerned to preserve a 'liberal' independence in his work, should yet, again and again, embody the virtues, essentially, of the Christian critical ideal.

[1] D. S. Savage, *The Withered Branch*, London, 1950, p. 15.

3

CRITICISM AS DIALOGUE

I

If Christian criticism may claim a relevant place within
'the common pursuit', we would expect no less in reverse:
that literary criticism should find a place within contemporary theological studies. The important ecumenical
symposium, *Theology and the University*,[1] exploring new
paths in theological education, recognizes the relevance
of literature for theology students by proposing that its
model course might include a seminar based on literary
texts. What follows is an attempt to give closer definition
to the rationale of such a seminar and to indicate the lines
on which it might develop.

The special excitement that a layman like myself, un-
trained in the disciplines of theology, may find in such
a seminar is inseparable from special difficulties and
dangers. It is not merely that the task of thinking about
such a course presses uncomfortably upon one's own
equipment, but that there is here so little experience to
draw on for nourishment or correction.

A complementary problem arises from the side of the
secular discipline upon which these studies are to be based.
As Fr Laurence Bright indicates in his proposals,[2] a number of disciplines, such as philosophy and sociology, might

[1] *Theology and the University*, ed. John Coulson, London, 1963.
[2] *Ibid.*, Chapter 11.

take their turn as the basis of this interdisciplinary course; and we may expect a lively resistance from within each discipline to anything that might seem to threaten a theological take-over bid. This of course is all to the good—including the good of theology; but it can be so difficult to maintain a proper autonomy, and to engage in mutually beneficial commerce, that a discipline may come to regard such interchanges with undue anxiety—reinforced, where relations with theology are concerned, by more special, radical suspicions. Such is certainly the case in contemporary literary studies; so that the committed Christian, concerned with literature, is often conditioned to keep his critical and theological interests safely apart, or at least to keep the latter well in the background.

That such a procedure can have important advantages is not in question. It certainly helps to keep imaginative writing in proper focus—to stress its peculiar integration of thought and feeling, of social and personal resources, its styles of linguistic embodiment, its elusive powers to nourish or debilitate—and to educate the literature student in appropriate modes of response. This is the basic dimension of literary-critical activity, and the task of defending and promoting these aims remains as vital as when Leavis and *Scrutiny* were first struggling to assert them. But while each generation has, we all know, in a sense to start again from the beginning, Leavis and his colleagues have now largely consolidated these aims. And it is for this very reason that we can now pertinently ask whether a literary criticism with these emphases may not, after all, be only a part—though of course always a central one—of critical assimilation; whether the assimilation of imaginative works does not finally require procedures beyond the 'analysis' and 'judgment'—the 'placing' within some order of creative importance—of individual works and writers. How far are these 'evaluating' activities, decisive as they are, designed (or intended) to grapple with those ultimate questions which can hardly be excluded from any fully serious encounter with imaginative visions—which may, or may not, be complementary, which may in fact be in radical tension with each other, and which may, or may not, cohere with our own prior beliefs and attitudes? Unless we are content to leave the deepest creative thinking of Hopkins and Yeats, Lawrence and Eliot, suspended as unco-ordinated forces within 'tradition', or in our own minds, we must put our trust in procedures, however hazardous, designed to bring them into dialectical relation. Assuming that *King Lear*, *Three Sisters* and *Waiting for Godot* all have some claim on our attention (however we assess their relative weight) may it not be profoundly relevant to question their visions, as partly converging, partly conflicting responses to tragic facts?[1] And how, in the end, can we avoid the task of exposing our social, or philosophical, or theological concerns to what we thus find ourselves addressed by, from the 'creative centre' of our culture?

Such dialectical tasks are, no doubt, quite especially hard to discipline—they are so dauntingly vast and open-ended—but since they cannot be disclaimed (only side-stepped) would it not be as well to come to terms with

[1] See Chapter 4 below.

the problems and risks inherent in their acceptance? And it is, after all, possible to proceed in this way while being constantly on one's guard against the external imposition of *a priori* theories and the reduction of works of art to illustrative conveniences. The aim must be to refocus the relations between imaginative works in terms of their own, fully respected integrity and weight—i.e. a genuine dialectical process, springing from genuine imaginative engagement. Accordingly, the underlying discipline remains that of textual analysis—and it is at this level that 'verification' must ultimately be sought; though there should be a growing interplay between unique imaginative forms and generic structures of feeling, between vision and vision, between intuitive and discursive modes of understanding. However careful we are, whatever precautions we take, the pitfalls will remain enormous. But, conscious of its legitimate dialectical tasks, criticism should thus feel free to point back, without apology, to the common experience and questions in which even works of genius are grounded—confronting their findings with each other, seeing our questions in theirs, putting our questions to their 'answers'.

I am stressing the needs within criticism for procedures we may call 'dialectical', both because these seem to me primary growing-points for criticism itself and because it is at these points that theology can most relevantly seek contact with it. It is most encouraging, from this point of view, to note how frontally L. C. Knights, in *Theology and the University*, stresses the *cognitive* functions of art and insists that—whatever the special characteristics of imaginative creativeness—there can finally be no essential discontinuity between art and other cognitive pursuits. 'Art matters', he says, 'not (certainly) because it indulges our feelings, not simply because it gives pleasure, but because it offers a form of knowledge.'[1] I cannot say how far Professor Knights would wish to subscribe to the conclusions I myself draw from this same basic conviction, how far a programme of 'dialectical criticism' would seem to him feasible. But that he would at any rate have some sympathy with the idea seems evident from his whole approach, and his conviction that 'the imagination is not a special faculty, but simply life coming to consciousness'.[2] And at one point, where he defends his own treatment of Shakespeare's plays, and especially of *King Lear*, against charges of 'killing the poetry in pursuit of an abstraction', his words could, without violence, be transposed into a foreword to the sort of critical procedures we are considering:

It seems that I must state the obvious and say that I do indeed regard *King Lear* as a great work of art, a highly wrought formal structure that engages our attention no less for the minutest parts than for the whole; no less for the precise way in which things are said and presented than for what we may call the substance. But what we call formal structure is not an end in itself; it is a means of simplifying, concentrating, enriching. When we attend to the play's 'organization as a work of art'—whether to such devices as the parallel plots and the juxtaposition of scenes or to the power and complexity of the spoken poetry—we find, inevitably, that we are dealing with *meanings* related one to another in a con-

[1] *Theology and the University*, ed. Coulson, p. 208.
[2] *Ibid.*, p. 217.

tinually widening context. These meanings of course are not definable units in a common currency (as when we speak of 'the dictionary meaning of a word'), they are thoughts, perceptions, feelings, evaluations that only exist for us in so far as, our minds and imaginations fully alert, we actively apprehend them, bring them home to such knowledge of ourselves and the world as we may already possess. If we do not so bring them home we may have some powerful feelings— whether about the harshness of the world or the grandeur and misery of man—but we are not exactly reading Shakespeare.[1]

Is it not evident that these finely distilled observations can be applied not only to a single work, but to a writer's entire creative career—and beyond this, to 'a continually widening context' of meanings, embracing all that is really meaningful to us? Inevitably, one thinks here of 'Tradition and the Individual Talent': 'No poet, no artist of any art, has his complete meaning alone'. But whereas for Eliot, when he wrote this, literature had more to do with emotion and 'the emotional equivalent of thought' than with any actual cognitive process, Professor Knights, seeing literature as 'a form of knowledge', insists that these related meanings 'only exist for us so far as, our minds and imaginations fully alert, we actively apprehend them, *bring them home to such knowledge of ourselves and the world as we may already possess*'. If even the 'reading' of a single work necessarily demands such a cognitive bringing home, how much more must be required from us as an indefinite multiplicity of—allied or rival—structures of meaning present themselves for assimilation. The individual work of art, however inexhaustibly rich in re-

[1] *Theology and the University*, ed. Coulson, pp. 213–14.

solved or unresolved problems or tensions, at any rate
consumes its own multiplicity in the unity of its form—
i.e. it is itself a dialectical structure; and so, perhaps, it
only needs to be re-created within ourselves to come
properly home to us. Similarly, in some cases—Shakespeare's, certainly, but also, for instance, Ibsen's or Yeats's,
or, for that matter, Eliot's own—a writer's entire development may form a dialectical unity that only awaits our
appropriation. But how are we to 'bring home' *as
knowledge*, to such knowledge as we may already possess,
the unorganized and indefinite, 'continually widening
context' of meanings among works and artists perhaps
creatively conscious of each other, perhaps mutually unaware, but in any case partners, be it as allies or rivals,
within the unity of our own awareness?

The answer, for the reader or critic, can only be either:
'Don't bother' or: 'Do it yourself'. And, as I see it, this
dialectical task is anything but an optional extra to other
steps towards bringing home the meaning of the meanings
we confront. Either we 'actively apprehend them' so that
they really become part of ourselves, a part of *our* knowledge; or we may have some powerful feelings—whether
about the harshness of the world or the grandeur and
misery of man—but we are not bringing home our
reading to such knowledge of ourselves and the world as
we may already possess. A mere jungle of meanings cannot take possession of the mind—except precisely *as* a
jungle, where meaning preys upon meaning without our
even noticing, or where the 'continually widening context' of meanings comes, in effect, to mean a progressive,

and perhaps ultimate, defeat of any meaningful orientation at all. The individual artist is engaged in an endless, 'intolerable wrestle/With words and meanings', to assert, or reassert, control over the jungle's endless encroachments:

> And so each venture
> Is a new beginning, a raid on the inarticulate
> With shabby equipment always deteriorating
> In the general mess of imprecision of feeling,
> Undisciplined squads of emotion.

The individual reader or critic, just because he himself lacks the equipment (however shabby) to raid the inarticulate, has to employ more indirect—and often more abstract—modes of assimilating the meanings which the great raiders, each for himself, have thus sought to establish or reclaim. Both the artist and critic are, it is true, nurtured and sustained by vast racial and cultural resources (without which there would, of course, not even be a jungle of meanings but only, literally, the jungle). Yet, finally, each man has to see, and hear, and answer for himself. He is answerable for the meanings he brings, or fails to bring, home. Thus it is only a measure of the seriousness with which we enter into imaginative writing to recognize that, finally, the kind of attention and questioning, the kind of readiness to live with, and live by, the meanings we are thus able to bring home, belongs most typically to faith—or the search for a faith; even though we may in fact be contemplating the resonances of 'panic and emptiness' or the celebration of a purely human glory. For at this depth of seriousness we can only aim at a homecoming from which no serious captured meanings are excluded; and although some of these meanings will, no doubt, organize themselves spontaneously around centres of insight below the discursive intelligence, whilst, conversely, one may simply be unable to fuse, or analyse, others into coherence, the *struggle towards* coherence, at every level of the mind, is crucial to the commitment to bring our captive meanings home. And although it is of course possible to be thus led to deny the final validity of theological significances, one could not, on these terms, skip urbanely over their 'hints and guesses'—

> echoed ecstasy
> Not lost, but requiring, pointing to the agony
> Of death and birth—

any more than one could stop one's ears to the echoing insinuations of Forster's Marabar Caves. At this depth, we must at least struggle towards a meaningful interaction between meaning and meaning, between awareness and awareness, between images announcing

> Thou hast one daughter
> Who redeems nature from the general curse
> Which twain have brought her to

and the tale told by the idiot, Lucky, in *Waiting for Godot*

that man in short that man in brief in spite of the progress of alimentation and defecation wastes and pines wastes and pines...

Only in such a struggle towards coherence amongst visions and fragments shored against our ruin can criticism strive to bring home the emergent implications of rival or complementary 'criticisms of life'.

Criticism as Dialogue

II

I have emphasized dialectical questioning as a discipline set in motion within the disciplines of the imagination itself, since it is on this plane that criticism inclines most insistently towards theological questions. Of course it is not only towards theology that the dialectics of the imagination are inclined; they may lead us anywhere where 'life coming to consciousness' may in fact tend. But at any rate it should be evident that theological forms of consciousness need not be external to critical activity, but may be struggling towards a foothold within the heart of literary experience itself. From this point of view, the activities of theology actually owe their relevance and urgency to our struggle towards consciousness amidst the facts and visions confronting the imagination.

Conversely, from the point of view of theology, literature represents the world of human existence—and the human commitment to self-understanding—to which 'the self-disclosure of God in Christ' is addressed '*as a present reality*'.[1] Literature is especially well equipped to represent man's historical experience to the theologian since, as Charles Davis notes, 'imaginative literature presents man in his changing situation, and it is man in the concrete who is the object of salvation'. Literature is needed by theology in the same sense in which Charles Davis speaks of theology needing the university. 'Notice', he says, 'that my plea is that theology needs the university, not that the university needs theology. As a matter of

[1] Charles Davis, in *Theology and the University*, ed. Coulson, p. 110.

fact the second statement is also true...But I am more concerned with the fact that theology itself needs the university. It needs the university so that it will ask the right questions, the questions that keep it at the growing points of human knowledge and within the consciousness of contemporary man.'[1]

But while it is vital to stress in this way theology's frequent, disabling failure to address the consciousness of contemporary man, to ask the right questions (or to ask them at a sufficient human depth)—so that literature must, in the first place, be allowed to probe the theologian's humanity, rather than be probed by his theological apparatus—it is no less pertinent that theological resources should be brought into play so far as literary experience may itself be reaching out towards some sort of theological awareness. In any case, judgment in literary matters is essentially a two-way process: a bringing home, and a going forth. He who responds is always (potentially at least) judged by what he responds to: that which claims our response always invites our judgment, precisely because it offers to judge us. What we are to bring home can, as we have seen, only be brought by way of the sort of imaginative dialectic that derives its impetus from the confrontation of meanings in tension. And what goes forth, to meet these interacting meanings, can only shed a relevant light in so far as it is directed precisely towards this dialectic. It is thus that literature may be said to need theology, no less than that theology needs literature: not to queen it over human darknesses and joys, but to enter

[1] *Ibid.*, p. 114.

divinely into them; not to prescribe from positions of pre-
fabricated strength, but as a probably rather suspect partner
in the common pursuit; seeking to place—not to displace
—the irreducible tensions and unanswerable questions
that will continue to probe us, far beyond our knowledge
or ease.

In the context of a seminar for theology students we
should, I believe, aim equally at educing this, potentially
highly creative—and in any case indispensable—unease,
and at leading the way towards pertinent forms of co-
operation with secular criticism. The reaction, voiced with
such force in *Theology and the University*, against the
'defensive-offensive' approach to the Christian apostolate
should, we may hope, take some of the shrillness out of
the secular–Christian dispute. It should—at any rate on
the Christian side—lead to something resembling the new
climate that has been achieved in inter-Christian discussions. And, as in ecumenical contexts, the most pressing
need is for a deepening understanding of each other's
vital commitments and more and more real awareness of
whatever is deficient in one's own. But it does not, of
course, follow that theology should now simply retire to
the receiving end. It remains, and cannot avoid remaining,
a voice crying in the wilderness, as well as an eye seeing
only as in a glass, and an ear attentive to neighbouring
voices. And in this sense the Christian reader or critic
cannot avoid being a theologian. Simply as a critic (I've
argued) he should in any case be concerned to engage the
meanings he enters in a dialectical inquisition, so that
they may truly enter into him. As a Christian, he cannot

avoid penetrating this dialectic with his faith—and so also, if appropriately respons've, exposing his faith to this dialectic. Thus, for the Christian student, literature studied in the context of theology should basically be just literature—met as a Christian, responding from within his faith, might anyway be expected to meet it, though perhaps with a more articulate theological emphasis. It should probe him, and probe his faith, as he probes—and seeks to place—*its* epiphanies. Anything more specifically 'theological' should, in this context, be secondary, or at any rate flow from this central activity.[1]

III

A seminar on these lines could of course take many different forms. It might examine a range of writing from a chosen historical period; or seek to trace continuities and

[1] Cf. Fr Herbert McCabe's account of the U.C.S. discussion booklet, *University Life*, p. 44: 'Our method...is the exact opposite of the conventional "Gospel Enquiry". This commonly begins with a reading from scripture, which is then analysed and applied to our ordinary experience, the final result being some practical conclusion. We have reversed this procedure. We begin with an examination of some aspect of university life—not at all with a view to "judging" it, or seeing how we can apply christian standards to it, but with a view simply to understanding it so that we can more fully enter into it. The second movement is to see the christian revelation as a depth within this human experience.'

The analogy with the suggested approach to literary studies is close; though, if I am right, 'understanding', 'entering into' and 'judging' are *inherently complementary* aspects of literary experience—so that Fr McCabe's 'second movement' of seeing 'the christian revelation as a depth within this human experience' is here not additional to the original experience and response but *simply the Christian's specific mode of dialectical engagement.*

changes as between two (or several) periods; or it might seek its focus directly in a cross-section of contemporary culture. Each of these patterns (and perhaps others) would have special advantages and might in fact be successively adopted; and each is, clearly, open to many variations. It is to be hoped that there would be a good deal of experimenting with different combinations and emphases.

I imagine, however, that—following from what has been said—there would be a deliberate effort to assimilate not only each text in its own right but their interrelations —with perhaps occasional pointers outwards, towards areas not directly represented among them. Secondly, as a corollary, the number of primary texts would need to be limited so as to facilitate real confrontation in depth, and so that students may be drawn in as increasingly active participants in the seminar's work. And, while it is vital to have some well-defined aims in directing discussions, a certain amount of improvisation might well be in place—even to the point of perhaps inserting an additional text here or there as discussions proceed. The seminar, as I understand it, is above all meant to arouse and cultivate certain habits of mind—habits at once 'academic' and deeply personal—and the tutor must feel his way—with *this* group, in *these* circumstances—as the seminar begins to take shape. In what follows I can only give some very sketchy indications of the kind of thing one might do.

My suggestions, here, are for a course offering a cross-section of contemporary culture. Bearing in mind the need to achieve a maximum representation of the directive forces at work, in terms of a minimum number of texts, I'd propose something like the following juxtapositions:

Lawrence: *The Rainbow* and *The Fox*.

Beckett: *Waiting for Godot*.

Brecht: *The Good Woman of Setzuan*.

Eliot: *Poems* and *The Cocktail Party*.

Lawrence would obviously have to be there, very much in the centre of any such course. And since *The Rainbow* (anyway one of his most important works) presents a picture of three generations, so as to arrive at its own diagnosis of modern culture in some historical depth, this seems a very suitable starting-point. As it happens, the novel offers some profound, direct challenges to Christian perspectives—or at least to what Lawrence, rightly or wrongly, takes to be Christianity's actual contribution to our culture. How far, we should inevitably find ourselves asking, are for instance Lydia Lensky's recurrent temptation to 'seek satisfaction in dread, to enter a nunnery, to satisfy the instincts of dread in her, through service of a dark religion', or Anna Brangwen's reflections, amidst the magnificences of Lincoln Cathedral, that 'God burned no more in that bush...She had always a sense of being roofed in'—how far are such passages merely relative to the characters concerned, how far do they express Lawrence's own sense of things; and—if the latter—how are we to bring their implications home? What lies behind them? What do they mean to *us*? (Here one might well refer to *Women in Love*, and especially the chapter called 'The Industrial Magnate', which poses the most deeply searching questions about the relations between natural human values and charity, and between Christian ideals of service and a destructive social activism.) Harder still, both because of its massive inherent complexities and because of the gaps and confusions in our own theological inheritance in these matters, how are we to respond to Lawrence's sex ethic? I'm not here thinking so much of the *Lady Chatterley* type of problem, which lies relatively near the surface, but of the multitude of elusive problems concerning the place of sex in maturely human lives, which Lawrence's art so largely exists to define. The more one reads a novel like *The Rainbow*, simply as a novel, the more one is likely to appreciate both the splendour and the deficient deployment of the Christian theology of marriage. At the same time, the more we have to learn from him, the more we have to be on our guard: only the deepest questioning can begin to disentangle what is finally valid for one, in Lawrence's embodied values, from what calls for qualification or resistance. Thus it is obviously impossible for a Christian to read Lawrence as he deserves to be read, without at the same time radically reconsidering not only the whole theology of sex but the place of sacrifice in human relations, and the place of natural fulfilment in the life of grace. This is why Lawrence is as indispensable to the professional theologian—even (perhaps especially) to the celibate moralist—as to the layman. True, Lawrence does not seem to think in terms of primary and secondary purposes, or actually offer instruction on family-spacing dilemmas, but—though we must always keep him distinct from the Catholic Marriage Advisory Council, and not confuse *The Rainbow* with manuals *De Castitate et Luxuria*—much of his work does, as a matter of fact, have bearings, maybe decisive bearings, even upon how these dilemmas ought to be approached.

Samuel Beckett is, in many ways, the exact antipode of Lawrence; and, although his standing is less assured, he is at least equally representative of the forces shaping the contemporary consciousness. Lawrence himself would, I suppose, have dismissed him in a contemptuous aside. He would *not* have appreciated the endlessly clowning cosmic belly-aches in *Waiting for Godot*, the self-conscious, cerebral equivocations and puzzles, Estragon's disconsolate question, 'What do we do now, now that we are happy?' Yet Beckett is on to something authentic; authentic, and no less humanly important than Lawrence's realized maps of fulfilment. Lawrence can show us, as only a very few can, how to fill temporal possibility to the brim. But because his demands on nature—nature as an ultimate, saving dimension—are absolute, as if men must regain Paradise by sheer purity of desire, he often seems to demand from human beings richnesses and strengths, and powers to fulfil each other, such as no man can, by taking thought, add to his stature (nor even by surrendering thought, to the disciplines of the *solar plexus*). What is to be done with the unfulfilled and unfulfilling—a Skrebensky, or a Hermione, or a Clifford Chatterley? Lawrence has little interest in this problem. More and more he seems simply to choose to take more and more literally Ursula's remark to her lover, Skrebensky: 'It seems to me...as if you weren't anybody—as if there weren't anybody there, where you are. Are you anybody, really? You seem like nothing to me.' And people who are literally nothing can be literally written off; for Lawrence they really are ultimately not there—least of all as objects of compassion. Unfortunately, the world (including Lawrence's world) is, in this sense, full of people who seem like nothing. They turn up again in Beckett. Indeed, Beckett's world is a world made safe for people who seem like nothing. They may, like Estragon, ask: 'What do we do now, now that we are happy?'; or boast: 'We don't manage too badly, eh, Didi, between the two of us?...We always find something, eh, Didi, to give us the impression that we exist?'; or they may surpass each other in shouting:

ESTRAGON   (*brandishing his fists, at the top of his voice*) God have pity on me!
VLADIMIR   (*vexed*) And me?
ESTRAGON   (*as before*) On me! On me! Pity! On me!

Yet they do have a claim on our pity—and may even be implicating us more directly—for all their ludicrous sub-existence. Even Pozzo, appallingly and grotesquely revolting though he is—monstrous even in his Second Act state of near-paralysis and blindness—finally (pressed to say since when Lucky had been dumb) is allowed the dignity of protesting:

Have you not done tormenting me with your accursed time? It's abominable. When! When! One day, is that not enough for you, one day like any other day, one day he went dumb, one day I went blind, one day we'll go deaf, one day we were born, one day we'll die, the same day, the same second, is that not enough for you: (*Calmer*) They give birth astride of a grave, the light gleams an instant, then it's night once more.

'That passed the time', Vladimir comments, as soon as Pozzo and Lucky have gone; but if we should be tempted to agree with Vladimir when he remarks elsewhere (obviously with one eye on the audience): 'This is becoming really insignificant', we need only turn back to Lawrence—his treatment of Clifford Chatterley, or, to a lesser extent, of Skrebensky, or his evident complicity in Banford's subconscious assassination, in *The Fox*—to recognize that Lawrence and Beckett are complementary, and that 'insignificance' has its own, profound significance in human affairs.

Lawrence and Beckett, then, are complementary, and each speaks to us with urgency; yet in the last resort they are incompatible. It is here that the task of distinguishing, and bringing home, those elements from each vision we finally wish to make our own becomes most pressing and exacting. Thus we are driven to ask how far Lawrence's demands for a purely natural self-fulfilment or even rebirth—particularly in the union of the sexes—can finally be assimilated to a faith grounded in the transcendence (as well as the immanence) of God, and in the doctrines of the Fall and Resurrection; or how far, on the other hand, Beckett's obsessive pre-occupation with human inadequacy can serve as a valid corrective to Lawrence's tendency to confuse immanence and transcendence.

Perhaps it will help to bring these questions into focus

to recall two or three more passages from *The Rainbow*, the first of which, though very well known, I should like to quote at some length:

Several letters, and then he was coming. It was Friday afternoon he appointed. She worked over her microscope with feverish activity, able to give only half her attention, yet working closely and rapidly. She had on her slide some special stuff come up from London that day, and the professor was fussy and excited about it. At the same time, as she focused the light on her field, and saw the plant-animal lying shadowy in a boundless light, she was fretting over a conversation she had had a few days ago with Dr Frankstone, who was a woman doctor of physics in the college.

'No, really', Dr Frankstone had said, 'I don't see why we should attribute some special mystery to life—do you? We don't understand it as we understand electricity, even, but that doesn't warrant our saying it is something special, something different in kind and distinct from everything else in the universe—do you think it does? May it not be that life consists in a complexity of physical and chemical activities, of the same order as the activities we already know in science? I don't see, really, why we should imagine there is a special order of life, and life alone—'

The conversation had ended on a note of uncertainty, indefinite, wistful. But the purpose, what was the purpose? Electricity had no soul, light and heat had no soul. Was she herself an impersonal force, or conjunction of forces, like one of these? She looked still at the unicellular shadow that lay within the field of light, under her microscope. It was alive. She saw it move—she saw the bright mist of its ciliary activity, she saw the gleam of its nucleus, as it slid across the plane of light. What then was its will? If it was a conjunction of forces, physical and chemical, what held these forces unified, and for what purpose were they unified?

78

For what purpose were the incalculable physical and chemical activities nodalised in this shadowy, moving speck under her microscope? What was the will which nodalised them and created the one thing she saw? What was its intention? To be itself? Was its purpose just mechanical and limited to itself?

It intended to be itself. But what self? Suddenly in her mind the world gleamed strangely, with an intense light, like the nucleus of the creature under the microscope. Suddenly she had passed away into an intensely-gleaming light of knowledge. She could not understand what it all was. She only knew that it was not limited mechanical energy, nor mere purpose of self-preservation and self-assertion. It was a consummation, a being infinite. Self was a oneness with the infinite. To be oneself was a supreme, gleaming triumph of infinity. [Ch. xv]

Here we have one of the vital keys to Lawrence's vision: his hostility to a conventional rationalism; the intent seriousness of concern with ultimate meanings that, in itself, gives his writing a religious dimension; and the explicit (and in *The Rainbow* insistent) preoccupation with what he calls 'the infinite'—or, as he has it elsewhere, 'the eternal'. 'To be oneself was a supreme, gleaming triumph of infinity'; and the sex-relation is, essentially, 'the doorway' to infinite otherness, to 'oneness with the infinite'. In this sense, self-fulfilment is not a liberty but a duty—perhaps the only absolute duty Lawrence recognizes—sharply contrasted with 'mechanical energy' and the 'mere purpose of self-preservation and self-assertion'.

Ursula's experience over the microscope, as she awaits Skrebensky's arrival, is a sort of Transfiguration. Everything else in the novel takes its bearings from here: 'Suddenly she had passed away into an intensely gleaming light of knowledge. She could not understand what it all was...Self was a oneness with the infinite.' It is Lawrence's commitment to this 'gleaming light of knowledge'—the depth and intensity, and richly dramatized exploration of this commitment—that raises his art to the unique position it holds in modern writing. But it is a commitment that has two corollaries which, it seems to me, finally compel us to put a limit to our endorsement. For, first, in spite of its emphatic distinction between the self as consummated into 'a being infinite' and the self as mere 'mechanical energy' and 'self-assertion', this self is, in both cases, merely the natural self—with the consequence that it can, at best, only transform mechanical self-assertion into a sort of sacred ethical egoism. And, secondly, this self is only capable of love and human compassion so far as the other person—by being himself (or herself) a natural conductor of 'infinity'—can consummate this sacred egoism. The passage we have been considering immediately continues:

Ursula sat abstracted over her microscope, in suspense. Her soul was busy, infinitely busy, in the new world. In the new world, Skrebensky was waiting for her—he would be waiting for her.

But Skrebensky fails as a natural conductor of 'infinity'; and, before long, he is cast out of her life—not with the sort of author's malice with which Lawrence was eventually to pursue Clifford Chatterley, or with which

Criticism as Dialogue

Banford is exterminated in *The Fox*[1]—but he does seem pretty well 'like nothing' when he disappears, anonymously married off, leaving Ursula reflecting:

> Did he belong so utterly to the cast-off past? She repudiated him. He was as he was. It was good he was as he was. Who was she to have a man according to her own desire? It was not for her to create, but to recognise a man created by God. The man should come from the Infinite and she should hail him...The man would come out of Eternity to which she herself belonged. [Ch. xvi]

The other passage I should like to recall is the description, early in the novel, of Lydia Lensky's slow and agonizing re-awakening to life, following a catastrophic past. It is a superb realization, in a kind of prose-poem, some nine or ten pages long, of a much-resisted resurrection of consciousness amidst the rhythms of the seasons and the demand for relationship by a stranger, Tom Brangwen— come out of Eternity (to which she herself no longer belonged). The whole passage should be closely examined, but here we can only note one or two of its connections with the self-and-infinity theme. Lydia's arousal from the death of which she fears to let go is paralleled by Tom's own hard struggle back towards positive life from the chaos and unbeing that her lapses 'into a sort of sombre exclusion' produce in him:

> He felt like a broken arch thrust sickeningly out from support. For her response was gone, he thrust at nothing. *And he re-*

[1] Cf. Ian Gregor's analysis, 'The Fox, A Caveat' (*Essays in Criticism*, January 1959); also Bernard Bergonzi's 'Literary Criticism and Humanist Morality' (*Blackfriars*, January 1962), which, very tellingly, indicates the significance of Lawrence's 'moral cripples'.

mained himself, he saved himself from crashing down into nothingness
from being squandered into fragments, by sheer tension, sheer
backward resistance. [Ch. ɪɪ; italics added.]

The triumph, in Tom and Lydia, of renewed life, as they
consummate each other's being with each other's destined
'infinity' is symbolically summed up in the giving way of
the 'broken end of the arch' to the rainbow image and a
new peace, overflowing towards Lydia's child:

She was no longer called upon to uphold with her childish
might the broken end of the arch. Her father and mother now
met to the span of the heavens, and she, the child, was free
to play in the space beneath, between. [Ch. ɪɪɪ.]

All this is magnificently done; and it will be evident how
it bears upon Ursula's revelation when she looks through
the microscope. And just as the 'infinity' Ursula is to
learn to live for merges into an essentially *natural* self-
fulfilment, so Lydia's and Tom's complementary rebirth
is essentially natural. Indeed, Lawrence emphatically distinguishes this rebirth from anything that might be taken
as a rebirth into *another* kind of life; and yet he goes out
of his way to stress the Christian parallel, actually talking
about a 'baptism to another life', 'the complete confirmation', and so on. Evidently he is concerned to offer this
sort of natural resurrection as an alternative to the religion
in whose bush God no longer burns for him. It is in the
course of these passages that Lydia is shown as insidiously
tempted 'to relapse into the darkness of the convent,
where Satan and the devils raged round the walls, and
Christ was white on the cross of victory'.

Lawrence, then, at one and the same time sets out to

affirm the sacredness and 'oneness with the infinite' of the properly realized self and to deny the transcendence of the 'Eternal'; and, similarly, to affirm an absolute need for a 'baptism to another life' and to deny both its sacrificial source and infinite *otherness*. It is as if Hopkins's *Windhover* were to be revised, so that 'brute beauty and valour and act, oh, air, pride, plume...' became the inmost subject of the poem, and the 'blue-bleak embers' which, 'ah my dear, / Fall, gall themselves, and gash gold-vermilion'—foreshadowing a risen glory—were to be ingeniously edited out, as a burnt-out anachronism.

But suppose now that a man or a woman struck down by some radical grief is unable to rise again in natural joy. Or suppose that they simply lack the natural gifts of joy. Or that the circumstances of their lives exact some crucial sacrifice. (Such suppositions are hardly eccentric.) What does Lawrence have to say to—or about—such lives? By the time he came to write *Lady Chatterley's Lover*, Lawrence expressed his awareness of this problem not merely by way of Clifford Chatterley's paralyzed legs but, explicitly, in Connie's reflection:

And dimly she realized one of the great laws of the human soul: that when the emotional soul receives a wounding shock, which does not kill the body, the soul seems to recover as the body recovers. But this is only appearance. It is really only the mechanism of the re-assumed habit. Slowly, slowly, the wound to the soul begins to make itself felt, like a bruise, which only slowly deepens its terrible ache, till it fills all the psyche. [Ch. v]

And Lawrence's response? It is all there in the novel's first sentence: 'Ours is essentially a tragic age, so we refuse to take it tragically.' In other words, Connie is to find resurrection with her game-keeper; while Clifford's 'terrible ache' is simply taken less and less seriously as the novel progresses. For such as him there is no hope of resurrection: only the contempt of the risen.

It is here—in Lawrence's inability to cope with incurable wounds and aches—and still more in his refusal to take them tragically—that his vision seems most gravely out of focus. The resulting disabilities range from moral to metaphysical distortions. It is hard to say whether his refusal of tragic compassion is the cause or the consequence of his refusal of tragic transcendence, whether his naturalistic reduction of the concepts of resurrection and salvation is the cause or the consequence of finding that 'God burned no more in that bush'. Either way, we are driven back to Beckett's counterpoise.

Here I must leave any further working out of the Lawrence–Beckett dialectic. There are of course vast ranges of material we have not begun to look into. Nor shall I here outline the ways in which Brecht and Eliot might impinge upon these discussions.[1] But I should like to remove a possible misapprehension.

Obviously there is a sense in which both Brecht and the later Eliot deliberately set out to offer 'solutions' to these problems. But we are dealing with works of art, not political or theological tracts. The proposed inclusion of *The Good Woman of Setzuan* in the seminar is, admittedly, in part, connected with Brecht's ideological representativeness; just as Eliot, and especially *Four Quartets*

[1] See Chapters 5 and 6, below.

and *The Cocktail Party*, so to speak, represent theology itself in the forum of secular culture. But the perspectives of Brecht's play reach out far beyond any such emphasis, impinging especially upon many aspects of Beckett (in relation to whom he seems almost as direct an antipode as Beckett, in turn, is to Lawrence). And Eliot, of course, has in any case an importance comparable to Lawrence's, and could hardly be kept out of such a course. In his case, I'd just like to stress that there should be no question of bringing him in as a sort of One-Eyed Riley, to dispose of all outstanding complications and problems. On the contrary, his inclusion should help to subject his own, theological imagination to the various counter-pulls of our other texts; and, as a matter of fact, I believe that *The Cocktail Party* is open to important critical and theological objections. Suffice it to note here that Dr Leavis, evidently picking his words for maximum economy, once said that there are two reviews of *The Cocktail Party* he would have been interested to see: one by D. H. Lawrence, and the other by Albert Schweitzer. We should, at any rate, be doing the next best thing in confronting *The Cocktail Party* with *The Rainbow* and Eliot's own *Quartets*.

4

THE EXTREME VERGE:
FROM TRAGEDY TO ABSURDITY

LEAR   I here take my oath before this honourable assembly,
      she kicked the poor king her father.
FOOL   Come hither, mistress. Is your name Goneril?
LEAR   She cannot deny it.
FOOL   Cry you mercy, I took you for a joint-stool.

Do we laugh, or do we weep? The question is perhaps
embarrassing in several ways, and we might want to cry
mercy and laugh it off. But we cannot deny it, she kicked
the poor king her father.

It is almost the Fool's last jest. He has nothing more to
say for the next thirty or forty lines, and then he goes to
bed at noon. There is nothing more to be said in his
terms. When, for instance, King Lear meets the blinded
Gloucester in the following act—'Ha! Goneril, with a
white beard!'—nobody intervenes. It is too late to
puncture the obsession, and anyway we can no longer,
even incipiently, summon the resources of laughter.
Laughter now sticks, not in our throat but in our chest;
and what swells up towards our heart cannot be knapped
o' the coxcombs with a 'Down, wantons, down!' And
so the Fool is withdrawn from the pressures and tensions
and dislocations of the play just as these arrive at their
fullness. Laughter remains latent within the play, but

pity and terror have finally disarmed it. Tragedy, pushed to a point where it violently presses upon the absurd, without itself collapsing, thus establishes its sovereignty over humour.

This it does once and for all. Some things are no laughing matter and they cannot be laughed off without cheating. There are wide—and sometimes unexpected—ranges of experience subject to laughter. Not only the laughter of sheer joy or celebration, or irony, from the most playful to the most severe. It is, of course, laughter that administers our common-sense values. There are abnormalities and follies which only laughter can properly grasp, and there are tensions and discords only laughter is equipped to release. Even sheer, unmitigated frustration can sustain a sort of laughter, and indeed cynicism has no other means of living but to eject the load again and again and again. What laughter cannot do is to abolish the ultimate seriousness of being alive, of having to choose and of having to die; and just as it cannot abolish the seriousness of these things, it cannot ultimately discharge their problems. It is only when it seeks to disown what it can neither abolish nor resolve that laughter ceases to be humane.

The Fool never cheats. His quips and verses—partly directed at Lear, partly towards ourselves—are all efforts of humaneness, within the limits of laughter. He does not cheat, but he fails. This failure is one of his main functions. Long before his final dismissal, the failure is complete. From the beginning, Lear had thought him a 'bitter fool', for he had shown him how much the rent of his land came to. But facts must be faced: that is the basic insistence of humour. To begin with, therefore, we laugh—and grow tenser and tenser as we laugh, since it is already too late to face facts. As we enter the storm, we are moved to laughter against such odds that these momentary sparks of sanity merely tickle our disintegration—

Prithee, nuncle, be contented, 'tis a naughty night to swim in.

By the time of Goneril's arraignment we hardly any longer know what a fact *is*, and the Fool's voice has lost all distinctness—

Cry you mercy, I took you for a joint-stool.

We are aware of a sort of surrealist pedantry struggling to cling to the cliffs of the mind, but its only effect is to make our brain turn.

In his classic essay on 'Lear and the Comedy of the Grotesque', Wilson Knight has suggested that, where *Macbeth* may be analogous to Dostoevsky, *Lear* is analogous to Chekhov:

To the coarse mind lacking sympathy an incident may seem comic which to the richer understanding is pitiful and tragic. So, too, one series of facts can be treated by the artist as either comic or tragic, lending itself equivalently to both. Sometimes a great artist may achieve significant effects by a criss-cross of tears and laughter. Tchehov does this, especially in his plays. A shifting flash of comedy across the pain of the purely tragic both increases the tension and suggests, vaguely, a resolution and purification. The comic and the tragic rest both on the idea of incompatibilities, and are also, themselves, mutually exclusive: therefore to mingle them is to add to the meaning of each: for the result is then but a new sublime incongruity.[1]

This relation between *Lear* and Chekhov, pertinent as it is in defining this sort of incongruity, may, however, be even more important in the differences it embodies. The 'criss-cross of tears and laughter' that makes up *The Seagull* or *Three Sisters* is certainly among the most significant inventions of modern art; but it is as far removed from the criss-cross of *Lear* as Dr Dorn and his Valerian drops are from the unavailing medicine of the Fool. Like the Fool, Dr Dorn dispenses the sanities of unillusioned common sense; and, like the Fool, he fails to arrest the mounting tensions, culminating in final catastrophe. But, whereas the Fool is violently funny throughout, shattering his laughter against the thunder, Dr Dorn's vein is gently ironic, and easily shifts to neutral tones. And whereas the Fool is brusquely liquidated at the height of the crisis, Dr Dorn literally has the last word: 'The fact is, Constantine has shot himself...'

It is a strange last sentence for a play sub-titled 'A Comedy'—though really no stranger than the whole complex of Chekhov's dramatic aims. For what is 'yoked by violence together' in *King Lear*, for a purely tragic purpose, Chekhov fuses and confuses till we scarcely know what it is we are moved to. Shakespeare shifts between the two poles with such high-charged rapidity, and suspends us so helplessly within the resulting tension, that he might almost seem to be *mingling* his tones, though

[1] *The Wheel of Fire*, London, 1930, reprinted 1941, p. 175.

The Extreme Verge

the total effect is in fact uncompromisingly tragic. In Chekhov, the two tones actually tend to dissolve into each other, and his plays are so elusive in their total impact that they have in fact occasioned endless disputes as to whether they should more properly be considered 'tragic' or 'comic'.

Comic, was Chekhov's own answer; and though we may disagree with him, we cannot ignore that this is what he thought. What is more, we cannot overlook the persistent return in the plays themselves to this sort of note:

SORIN   Where's my sister?

DORN   Gone to the station to meet Trigorin, she'll be back any moment.

SORIN   If you felt my sister had to be sent for, I really must be ill. [*After a short pause.*] It's a funny thing—I'm seriously ill, but I don't get any medicine.

DORN   What would you like? Valerian drops? Soda? Quinine?

SORIN   Oh, the speeches have started. This is the limit. [*Nods towards the sofa.*] Is that bed for me?

POLINA   Yes.

SORIN   Thank you.

DORN   [*Singing softly.*] 'See the moon floating by in the evening sky.'

SORIN   I'd like to give Constantine a plot for a novel. It ought to be called *The Man who Wanted—L'homme qui a voulu*. In youth I wanted to become a writer—I didn't. I wanted to speak well—I spoke atrociously. [*Mocks himself.*] 'And all that sort, er, of thing, er, don't yer know.' I'd be doing a summing-up sometimes, and find myself jawing on and on till I broke out in a sweat. I wanted to marry—I didn't. I wanted to live in town all the time—and here I am ending my days in the country and so on.

DORN You wanted to become a senior civil servant—and
did.

SORIN [*Laughs.*] That's one thing I wasn't keen on, it just
happened.

DORN To talk about being fed up with life at the age of
sixty-two—that's a bit cheap, wouldn't you say?

SORIN Don't keep on about it, can't you see I want a bit of
life?

DORN That's just silly. All life must end, it's in the nature
of things.

SORIN You're spoilt, that's why you talk like this. You've
always had what you wanted, so life doesn't matter to
you, you just don't bother. But even you'll be afraid of
dying.

DORN Fear of death's an animal thing, you must get over
it. It only makes sense to fear death if you believe in
immortality and are scared because you've sinned. But
you aren't a Christian for a start, and then—what sins
have you committed? you've worked for the Department
of Justice for twenty-five years, that's all.

SORIN [*Laughs.*] Twenty-eight.[1]

This is the classic remedy of comic wisdom (and not
only of comic). *Such is life. No pills for earth-quakes.*
'Valerian drops? Soda? Quinine?':

> He that has a little tiny wit,
>   With hey, ho, the wind and the rain,
> Must make content with his fortunes fit,
>   Though the rain it raineth every day.

But what gives Chekhov his peculiar importance is his
equally persistent refusal to provide comic relief (the

[1] *The Seagull*, Act IV. Quotations from Chekhov are from Ronald
Hingley's translations in *The Oxford Chekhov*, volumes II and III,
London, 1964 and 1967.

phrase calls for rescue) without fully confronting the misery of things. So radical and compassionate is his penetration of human defeat that it is this aspect of his work that most attracts the focus of attention. And rightly, for it is here that *the terms* of his vision are disclosed. These terms are largely akin to those of tragedy: the problem he has set himself is essentially the tragic problem.

Yet the emerging vision is not tragic—though it may easily appear so. It is neither tragic in the sense that, say, *The Bacchae* or *The Duchess of Malfi* or *The Father* might be called tragic—a cry of protest or despair; nor in the sense in which *The Oresteia* or *King Lear* or *Brand* might be so called—where desperation is somehow transcended from within, through the tragic experience itself.

At the same time, however, it is not a truly comic vision either, in spite of Chekhov's explicit aim. We need not ask whether he meant 'comic' to carry an ironic over-tone. Sorin's predicament (though he is of course a minor figure) and Dr Dorn's manner of responding are a sufficient index of where Chekhov meant to go. Nearly everybody in Chekhov is a Man who Wanted, though some may have wanted a bit more cheaply than others. That makes for a limited tragic pattern—tragic in the line of *Hamlet*—suitably reduced, of course, to Waste Land proportions:

> ...But you aren't a Christian for a start, and then— what sins have you committed? You've worked for the Department of Justice for twenty-five years, that's all.

But the pattern is not only diminished; clinched by this final irrelevancy, it is twisted into a comic look. Again and again we encounter this twist. Often it is a deliberate jest, as it is here. Often it resides in the characterization, or in absurdities of juxtaposition. It may be downright funny or obliquely caressing; it may break explosively from unbearable tension, or be teased out with delicate, marginal deliberation. Even the most recalcitrant material yields to this touch, as with Uncle Vanya's horrifying and heartrending attempt to shoot the professor. The touch is masterly, but it leaves us in confusion. And it is hard to accept the emerging vision as comic, in any sense.

It fails to be comic precisely because of Chekhov's integrity. Once again Dr Dorn and a very minor figure pinpoint the problem. In the abstract, the tangle of re-lationships in *The Seagull* has almost the potentialities of farce: Medvedenko, the school-master, is desperately in love with Masha—who desperately worships Constan-tine—whose love for Nina is to be reduced to despair when Nina falls for Trigorin, the successful if second-rate novelist—who is to leave her in abandoned desolation. On top of this, Masha's mother, Polina, jealously pursues Dr Dorn; whilst Irina Arkadin (Constantine's mother) equally jealously hangs on to Trigorin; thereby not only causing him to abandon Nina, but completing the defeat of her somewhat mother-fixated son. (For good measure, there is also the complex and indeed primary theme of artistic vocation and failure.) There could hardly be a stronger groundwork for sheer comic absurdity, but what emerges is—well—'Chekhov'. At the end of the First Act, Constantine exits hysterically and Dorn is left alone with Masha:

DORN [*with a sigh.*] Ah, to be young!

MASHA When people can't think what to say they always hold forth about the young. [*Takes some snuff.*]

DORN [*takes the snuff-box off her and hurls it into the bushes.*] That's disgusting. [*Pause.*] I think someone's playing the piano indoors. I must go in.

MASHA Just a moment.

DORN What is it?

MASHA I must tell you again, I must speak. [*Excitedly.*] I don't care for my father, but I have a soft spot for you. Somehow we have so much in common, I feel it with all my heart. So help me. Help me, or else I'll do something silly and make a mess of my life, ruin it. I can't go on.

DORN Meaning what? How can I help you?

MASHA I'm so unhappy. No one, no one knows how I suffer. [*Lays her head on his breast, softly.*] I love Constantine.

DORN What a state they're all in. And what a lot of loving. Oh, magic lake! [*Tenderly.*] But what can I do, my child? What can I do?

CURTAIN

This curtain line seals the defeat of comedy no less surely than did the dismissal of Lear's fool. Masha is perfectly right: 'When people can't think what to say, they always hold forth about the young.' (Or they can cry 'That's disgusting'.) What, however, gives this scene its special importance is that Dorn is, for once, swept off his poise. His irony gasps, wobbles and gives way. Then his curtain line snapshots the impotence beneath his ironic entrenchment.

But the confession is filed away, and the play proceeds

without further hesitation along its course, right up to that
other—final—curtain when Dorn whispers the news:

Get Irina out of here somehow. The fact is, Constantine has
shot himself.

It is a terrible announcement, but—just as he had resisted
the conventionally comic—Chekhov refuses to take it
tragically. It is almost as if he himself were saying over
again 'Ah, to be young!' (But what can he do? What
can he do?) He wants to get us out of here somehow—he
is not Strindberg. But where are we to be taken? 'A
shifting flash of comedy', says Wilson Knight, 'across
the pain of the purely tragic both increases the tension
and suggests, vaguely, a resolution and purification.' It
does; but in the last resort you can only resolve the re-
solvable; and some things are resistant to comic resolution. These things elude the laughter of the Fool, and
they elude the irony of Dr Dorn. But the Fool capitulates;
Dr Dorn holds on. The Fool faces facts—including the
fact of his failure. Dr Dorn faces facts, and returns to his
drops. It is perfectly true that, both in *Lear* and in *The
Seagull*, the criss-cross of tragedy and comedy both increases the tension and suggests a resolution; but only
Lear finally sustains what it suggests. Chekhov will have
neither ultimate desperation nor tragic release. In the last
resort, therefore, he retreats to his special brand of comic
relief—to an irony deprived of its backbone. In this
irony—whose apparent standards of reference are themselves subjected to irony—we lose our bearings and,
having lost them, can feel that something has been re-

solved. For all Chekhov's integrity, we are finally cheated. He has given us his authoritative diagnosis; he has required us to face facts, and exhorted us to courage; but he finally obliges us to swallow a medicine he can only prescribe with irony.

II

Why does Chekhov cheat? Why will he not accept the limits of comic resources? The question takes us not only to the core of Chekhov's own art, but is a test-question for a very large sector of modern writing.

Chekhov's tone is, of course, a highly personal achievement, but at the same time it is typical of our age. It is, in fact, the prototype of a large family of tones dominant in modern writing, ranging from Synge and O'Casey and, for instance, E. M. Forster (for it extends far beyond the theatre) to Brecht and Giraudoux, and perhaps even *The Cocktail Party* and *The Confidential Clerk*. It is clearly a major index of our time; and it is doubtful whether anyone has equalled Chekhov's mastery of its possibilities.

We may assume, then, that what limits Chekhov's achievement in this manner are the limitations inherent in the manner itself. These limitations derive from the very nature of the undertaking—to impose a 'comic' resolution upon essentially tragic material. For, as we have seen, what distinguishes Chekhov's kind of tonal synthesis from Shakespeare's is precisely that inversion whereby *comedy* is given the task of ultimate resolution. That one or the other tone *must* be dominant (unless we are content with a mere hotch-potch) is implicit in that sentence of Wilson Knight's in our quotation where he says that 'the comic and the tragic rest both on the idea of incompatibilities, *and are also themselves mutually exclusive*' (my italics). In the end, one or the other must prevail, or the 'new sublime incongruity' produced by their conjunction will expend itself in sheer incoherence. Chekhov plumps for comedy; and the result is inevitably a measure of distortion.

Inevitably—for there are only three sorts of ways in which comedy can be offered as the dominant element in a synthesis of tones: (i) it may dominate by virtue of a *limitation* of tragic elements (as, for instance, with the Hero-theme in *Much Ado*); (ii) or by a *distancing* of tragic elements (as in *The Winter's Tale* or *The Cocktail Party*); (iii) or by asserting an inherent *subordination* of the tragic towards the comic (which is what we found in *The Seagull*). The first two of these may be the result of purely conventional restrictions (similar to those of comedy pure and simple)—in which case they need occasion no problem; or else are symptoms of an underlying failure of vision (as, for instance, the shirking of tragic realities by Bernard Shaw). The third kind of mode, asserting the ultimate sufficiency of a comic response to life, is simply asserting what is not the case; and it can only do this in terms of some measure of trickery—or convert itself into a deliberate, absurdist self-cancellation.

In Chekhov this takes several forms. In *The Seagull* we can locate it in the manœuvres of Dr Dorn. In *Three Sisters*—his most splendid achievement—there is no such focus, and only a detailed analysis of the entire pattern could pin-point the infirmities of its vision. Something of its central unsteadiness can, however, be sampled from a glance at the final tableau, when all the concrete hopes and compensations painfully acquired during the play have foundered, and the sisters are left behind, no longer even in possession of their house, with the military band that is taking away Vershinin playing a 'rousing' march off-stage. The ironies—harvesting all the ironies that have gone before—clash against each other like a confrontation of mirrors, as the sisters face the necessity to go on living and dream of those who will come after them—

But our sufferings will bring happiness to those who come after us, peace and joy will reign on earth, and there will be kind words and kind thoughts for us and our times—

just as Vershinin had dreamed throughout the play. Meanwhile their brother crosses the stage, wheeling the baby his vulgar, adulterous wife can no longer be bothered with, and Chebutykin softly sings his 'Tararaboomdeay, let's have a tune today', as he reads his paper and adds 'None of it matters. Nothing matters', for the last time; leaving Olga to her final 'If we could only know, oh if we could only know!'. Triumphant as this is as a dramatic finish, the *catharsis* it achieves depends upon the vaguest and most unsubstantial fantasies—which the play itself has, many times, teased—and is teasing again, defensively, even as it invites us to accept them as ultimate means of resolution. Only, this time there is no Dr Dorn— how right Chekhov was to withhold a successor!—to confess the ironic illusionism that is being practised. In his last play, *The Cherry Orchard*, the irony is more vertebrate. But if Chekhov thus comes much nearer to imposing a genuine 'comic' resolution, it is at the price of scaling down the tragic challenge he now set himself. It is as if, firmly determined to *substantiate* his non-tragic optimism (somewhat along the lines E. M. Forster was to attempt in *Howards End*), he had been driven to a corresponding withdrawal from tragic exposure.

One work stands outside this account: *Uncle Vanya*, written between *The Seagull* and *Three Sisters*. For in this work it is the comic element that at last gives way. No attempt is finally made to allow us any sort of temporal hope; Voynitsky's words, as he looks up from his accounts, have all the weight of the play behind them:

I'm so depressed, Sonya, you can't think how depressed I feel.

Sonya's response begins like Masha's 'We must go on living, we must' (on the face of it, the situation is very similar to the conclusion of *Three Sisters*):

Well, it can't be helped. Life must go on.

But, after a pause, she continues:

And our life will go on, Uncle Vanya. We shall live through a long succession of days and endless evenings. We shall bear patiently the trials fate has in store for us. We shall work for others—now and in our old age—never knowing any peace. And when our time comes we shall die without complaining. In the world beyond the grave we shall say that we wept and suffered, that our lot was harsh and bitter, and God will have pity on us. And you and I, Uncle dear, shall behold a life which is bright and beautiful and splendid. We shall rejoice and look back on our present misfortunes with feelings of tenderness, with a smile. And we shall find peace. We shall, Uncle, I believe it with all my heart and soul. [*Kneels down in front of him and places her head on his hands, continuing in a tired voice.*] We shall find peace.

[TELEGIN *quietly plays the guitar.*]

We shall find peace. We shall hear the angels, we shall see the sky sparkling with diamonds. We shall see all the evils of this life, all our own sufferings, vanish in the flood of mercy which will fill the whole world. And then our life will be calm and gentle, sweet as a caress. I believe that, I do believe it. [*Wipes away his tears with a handkerchief.*] Poor, poor Uncle Vanya, you're crying. [*Through tears.*] There's been no happiness in your life, but wait, Uncle Vanya, wait. We shall find peace. [*Embraces him.*] We shall find peace.

[*The watchman taps.*]

[TELEGIN *quietly strums.* MRS VOYNITSKY *writes something in the margin of her pamphlet.* MARINA *knits her stocking.*] We shall find peace.

THE CURTAIN SLOWLY FALLS

Now, what is astonishing about this passage is not simply that it is 'tragic', but that it is false. Nowhere else in the plays do we encounter anything comparable. The threadbare rhetoric of Sonya's speech dispenses consolation with a vengeance. Its sentimental effect is, moreover, greatly increased by the fact that the speech is so largely unrelated to what has gone before: there have been a few incidental references to religion, but nothing that might have prepared us for this sort of thing. Yet, apart from this ending, the quality of the writing is second only to *Three Sisters*. Something must have badly dislocated Chekhov's poise to cause such a failure of tact. We can only assume that he was exerting himself to achieve, at all costs, an effect essentially alien to him.

Alternatively, Sonya's speech could be taken as a climactic structural irony. In these terms, the speech rings false since it rests upon illusion—and is meant to come through as manifesting illusion: bravely compassionate—in a sense fully rising to the occasion—and yet a symptom of ultimate bankruptcy. Thus the essential effect would be to turn the very gestures of comfort into a measure of 'the evils of this life'—confirming the sense of sheer, irreversible dereliction.

Yet the latter part of the speech is, after all, sustained by Telegin's 'quiet' playing of the guitar; which—despite the old nurse's helpless recourse to her knitting and Mrs Voynitsky's invincible absorption in her pamphlet—can hardly fail to control us, in the theatre, with its conclusive harmonies, underpinning Sonya's promises of 'sweetness' and 'peace'.

And so perhaps what finally lingers is precisely a clash of mutually exclusive implications apparently harmonized, parallel to the end of *Three Sisters*. Only here the consolatory note is at once more desperately assertive and more desperately unestablished as a metaphysical assertion. Gestures towards a transfigured secular future (whether cumulatively self-cancelling, as in *Three Sisters*, or residually intact, as in *The Cherry Orchard*) can at any rate be accommodated within the dimension of Chekhov's poetic naturalism; gestures towards eternity can only emerge beyond the limits of his idiom—or be reclaimed as naturalistic ironies.

We can see now why Chekhov strove so hard to keep his drama 'comic', far beyond the limits of comedy. 'We must go on living, we must'. Chekhov the artist, like Chekhov the doctor, was toughly determined to fight on the side of life, in the teeth of defeat and desperation and death. All around him the decay of his world was quickly advancing, and he saw it as his task to continue to say Yes. But he could not say Yes without cheating, since only a tragic resolution can resolve tragic facts; and tragic resolutions were beyond him. Chekhov was fully open to the facts. And, in his own terms, he could be as potent an exponent of the unbearable as Strindberg or the Ibsen of *Ghosts*. But he would neither content himself with a mere expression of shock, nor retreat into irrelevant side-shows. And he could not lay hold on tragic *catharsis*. He could only push his genius into ironic substitute-resolutions:

> —None of it matters. Nothing matters.
> —If we could only know, oh if we could only know!

Chekhov's predicament is the predicament of our age.

III

When Shakespeare drops the Fool, Poor Tom is already in the process of taking over:

> First let me talk with this philosopher.
> What is the cause of thunder?

And, although he does not like the fashion of his garments, Lear entertains him for one of his hundred. The Fool had led the king to the beginnings of charity and madness: Poor Tom is the thing itself. And, as Edgar rises through his representative series of transformations—unaccommodated man, peasant, soldier, knight, earl, king—his structurally privileged position becomes more and more assured:

Ripeness is all.

At the same time, Cordelia, hopelessly absent for so long, slowly returns to the play: first by report; then in person; and finally in death. Between them, they crystallize the emerging vision of the play.

Comedy has been interred. Horror is in ascendance, and the pity of it seems unredeemable:

Never, never, never, never, never!

Have we been brought all this way—through tempest and madness, through blindness and restoration:

Upon such sacrifices, my Cordelia,
The gods themselves throw incense—

only for that final vicious twist:

The gods defend her!...

Enter LEAR *with* CORDELIA *dead in his arms*—?

Do we conclude, with Swinburne, that 'the darkness of revelation is here'?[1] Or, as William Empson has said, that the core of the play is 'a fundamental horror, an idea that the gods are such silly and malicious jokers that they will soon destroy the world'?[2] Or even assimilate *Lear* to *Endgame*, as Jan Kott does?[3]

[1] A. C. Swinburne, *A Study of Shakespeare*, London, 1880, p. 172.
[2] William Empson, *The Structure of Complex Words*, London, 1951, p. 156.
[3] Jan Kott, *Shakespeare our Contemporary*, London, 1964, Chapter 6.

The Extreme Verge

Wilson Knight, R. B. Heilman and John F. Danby are among those who have most effectively demonstrated the inadequacy of such conclusions.[1] In some ways, however, the most telling witness, in this connection, is perhaps I. A. Richards. His well-known passage on tragedy, in *Principles of Literary Criticism*,[2] specifically instances *Lear* as a tragedy issuing in *catharsis*—'that sense of release, of repose in the midst of stress, of balance and composure' which tragedy at its greatest occasions. If he is right—and surely he is—if this is the kind of experience we are left with by *King Lear*, we are entitled to ask how this should be. What is there to 'repose' in, as Lear dies of his 'never's?

Dr Richards himself answers this question in terms of his psychological aesthetics: it is all a matter of organizing our 'impulses' into a fully inclusive poise. 'The joy which is so strangely the heart of the experience is not an indication that "all's right with the world" or that "somewhere, somehow, there is Justice"; it is an indication that all is right here and now in the nervous system'. One cannot help feeling that this is placing rather a strain on our nerves; the joy to which Dr Richards is referring surely cannot be as strange as *that*. Most of us simply are not reduced to solipsism as we enter a theatre, and most of us care about the nature of our world. So, as a matter of fact, does Dr Richards himself. For almost immediately

[1] G. Wilson Knight, *The Wheel of Fire*, London, 1930; R. B. Heilman, *This Great Stage: Image and Structure in 'King Lear'*, Lousiana State University, 1948; John F. Danby, *Shakespeare's Doctrine of Nature*, London, 1949. I have also learned much from D. G. James' *The Dream of Learning*, London, 1951 and D. A. Traversi's articles in *Scrutiny*, vols. XIX, no. 1—XIX, no. 3, 1952–3.

[2] I. A. Richards, *Principles of Literary Criticism*, London, 1924, pp. 245–6.

he adds: 'Tragedy is only possible to a mind which is for the moment agnostic or Manichean. The least touch of any theology which has a compensating Heaven to offer a tragic hero is fatal.' We shall turn to this question in a moment; the immediate point is simply that, in spite of Dr Richards's almost Swinburnian view, he witnesses to a joy we may be surprised by at the heart of the play.

A joy discovered at the heart of a fundamental horror is certainly a challenging experience. Indeed, since this 'horror' explicitly involves the ultimate nature of things—

As flies to wanton boys are we to the gods...

—the emergence of 'joy' as we contemplate the tragic image is just about the most important sort of experience men can have. It is possible to wrestle with such an experience and be left in perplexity; but one cannot do less, without self-violation.

One thing that can be done towards coming to better grips with it, is to free oneself of *a priori* assumptions. Among these, the most important is perhaps the idea that ' the least touch of any theology which has a compensating Heaven to offer a tragic hero' must be fatal to tragedy. Dr Richards is by no means alone in holding this view; it is a very widely held view indeed. It is shared, for instance, by such different writers as Karl Jaspers[1] and D. D. Raphael,[2] and is presupposed, in a qualified form, by Miss Una Ellis-Fermor, in her important essay 'The Equilibrium of Tragedy'.[3] Now, on this plane, it need only

[1] Karl Jaspers, *Tragedy is Not Enough*, London, 1952, pp. 38–40.
[2] D. D. Raphael, *The Paradox of Tragedy*, London, 1959, pp. 37–68.
[3] Una Ellis Fermor, *The Frontiers of Drama*, London, 1945, pp. 127–47.

be shown that, while many tragic works do indeed imply an 'agnostic or Manichean' vision, this is not a necessary condition of tragic experience. The idea that 'the least touch of any theology which has a compensating Heaven to offer' to the hero is fatal presupposes that tragedy must always be irredeemably fixed in outrage. But while there are many tragedies answering such a description, tragedy at its greatest—issuing in 'that sense of release, of repose in the midst of stress, of balance and composure' to which Dr Richards pays tribute—cannot be thus prejudged before we start. Indeed, as Dr Richards insists, the essential claim of a work like *Lear* upon us is precisely that the evil it images is somehow transcended; so that, unless we are content to pass it all off as just a marvellous psychological trick, 'the joy which is so strangely the heart of the experience' must be the index of some sort of real, relevant apprehension, beyond mere outrage.

What, then, is the meaning of this terrible joy? Once we have cleared away facile psychological reductions and *a priori* blue-prints of what tragedy can do, we are free to respond to the mystery of the play's *catharsis*. What we are searching for—

We had the experience but missed the meaning—

has the clarity and obscurity of a painting or a human face—a vision 'not lost, but requiring'. It is here, in the play, but not only in the play. We cannot confront the image without facing the fact; and fact and image require us to meet them (if ever the phrase had any validity) with our reasons of the heart:

What is the cause of thunder?

The *reasons* of the heart. So essentially 'rational' is this inquest that *Lear* has its own metaphysical method, a method as rigorous as Descartes's, and vastly more radical: the method of despair. Other tragedies may engulf us in desperation: *Lear* systematically strips us of value, till we unbutton the last of our lendings, and finally strangles our slowly reviving hope with: *Enter* LEAR, *with* CORDELIA *dead in his arms.*

This, above all, is why we have the Fool. The Fool is there to ensure that every conceivable alternative to despair shall be given its chance, and then slain—so that despair shall be all the more absolute (just as Descartes postulated his error-addicted daemon to ensure a sufficiently radical doubt). But whilst Descartes smuggled back, through his *cogito*, what an absolute doubt cannot allow, Shakespeare reveals the rebirth of hope within a truly absolute despair.

Lear is not *Timon* or *Troilus*. Its cumulative reductions and annihilations—its madnesses and blindnesses and desperations and heart-breaks—the very word 'nothing' echoing and re-echoing throughout the play—are all big with their absolute opposites; and it is in an exactly opposite sense from Timon's that this anguished world might cry:

> And nothing brings me all things.

We can view this emergent mystery in the microcosm of the mock-suicide scene. The symbolic immediacy of the cliff that isn't there—

> How fearful
> And dizzy 'tis to cast one's eyes so low—

embraces much more than Gloucester's personal experience. In its context, it also stands proxy for Lear's—who has been physically absent since the Fool's liquidation, and is presently to reappear at his most lunatic and most profound; and indeed it distils the entire tragic rhythm of the play.

For this scene not merely compresses the movement from sheer despair—

> you are now within a foot
> Of the extreme verge—

to acceptance (through Gloucester) of Edgar's unconditional commitment to 'free and patient thoughts':

> henceforth I'll bear
> Affliction till it do cry out itself
> 'Enough, enough', and die.

It obliquely *interprets* this movement, in terms of Gloucester's 'blindness'. Gloucester, deceived and betrayed by Edmund—as he had once been deceived by the 'sport at his making'—is now once more suffering deception:

GLOUCESTER Methinks the ground is even.
EDGAR   Horrible steep:
　　Hark! do you hear the sea?
GLOUCESTER   No, truly.
EDGAR Why then, your other senses grow imperfect
　　By your eyes' anguish.
GLOUCESTER   So may it be indeed.
　　Methinks thy voice is altered, and thou speakst
　　In better phrase and manner than thou didst.
EDGAR You're much deceiv'd; in nothing am I chang'd
　　But in my garments.

Even in saying this, Edgar is deceiving him; and yet he
is merely telling the truth. For indeed Gloucester is 'much
deceived'—much, much deceived: more than ever in his
present despair—and there *are* cliffs of fall before his feet.
Edgar's 'deceptions' are thus themselves deceptive: in
reality they are not deceptions at all—he remains the thing
itself throughout his transformations—but the truth.

The complexity of this situation exactly corresponds
to the complex revelatory rhythm of the play as a whole
(just as its compound of absurdity and tragic force reflects
its general tone). Under Edgar's supervision, Gloucester's
blindness is turning into a sort of seeing:

> Thy life's a miracle

Edgar assures him; and surely it is?

> Look up a-height; the shrill-gorg'd lark so far
> Cannot be seen or heard: *do but look up*.

Of course, he knows very well that Gloucester will have
to reply:

> Alack! I have no eyes.

But there is nothing cruel or unnecessary about his ex-
hortation. Gloucester is ready, at last, to assent:

> Think that the clearest gods, who make them honours
> Of men's impossibilities, have preserved thee.

And, in his blindness—'I see it feelingly', as he later tells
Lear—he *sees*:

> henceforth I'll bear
> Affliction till it do cry out itself
> 'Enough, enough', and die.

What Edgar thus points to, and Gloucester painfully grasps, is among the play's central 'reasons of the heart'; while, at the same time, it defines the very nature of such 'reasons'. The very 'cruelty' of the scene—whose apparent gratuitousness has so often been taken as its essential meaning—is in fact the tragic surpassing of cruelty: tragedy pushed beyond mere tragic outrage. If it is 'cruel', it is cruel only as *Job* is cruel (since the facts of tragic experience are cruel). If affliction *must* be borne—and the play makes *us* see that it must—the world ceases to be bottomlessly absurd.

The mere fact of moral exposure—exposure to that ultimate imperative that denies a man the choice of death—even as it seems to seal his cosmic entrapment, indicates a measure of shelter: shelter from the maddening image of Tom, the thing, shelter from manhood stripped of manhood: shelter from ultimate exposure to 'nothing'. To this extent, Chekhov also—'We must go on living, we must'—transcends desperation, as we have seen. *Lear* descends more deeply into the heart's mind; and it is the depth of its penetration of 'patience' that releases the play's tragic joy.

For 'patience', here, is not simply a moral achievement: essentially, it is an insight into existence. It is the practical acknowledgment—partly the seed, partly the fruit—of a cosmic apprehension, an incipient apprehension of the cause of thunder. 'Ripeness is all' thus implies a whole order of things—that ultimate order that has been put to the test by the play, an order in which there is *meaning*—even (perhaps even especially) in afflic-

tion and heartbreak and death, and in which it makes
sense to say:

> Upon such sacrifices, my Cordelia,
> The gods themselves throw incense.

Lear shows that this makes sense, however strangely.
And it shows this with all the more assurance by not
merely confronting us with 'the worst', but by finally
abandoning us to a conclusion in which the worst has
the last—gratuitously terrible last—word. Not only is
there—as Empson has it—that parting 'crack at the gods',

> The gods defend her!...

> *Enter* LEAR *with* CORDELIA *dead in his arms*

but (again in Empson's words): 'Lear is now thrown back
into something like the storm phase of his madness...The
last time he talked about unbuttoning was when he tore
off his clothes to be like the naked beggar, in search of
the rockbottom which is the worst. There is no worst; the
only rockbottom he can find is the grave, and it is a release. In the next two lines he dies of a passion of joy at
the false belief that Cordelia has recovered.'[1] This crown-
ing illusion, Empson feels, completes the 'fundamental
horror' of the play.

Its horror is indeed as radical as any ever shown forth.
And Empson is entirely right so far as he goes: in a sense
this is what we are left with. And yet, the play as a whole
has prepared us for a more inclusive response—in which

[1] *The Structure of Complex Words*, p. 152.

nothing of all this is disowned, but it is all tragically transcended:

> Thou hast one daughter
> Who redeems nature from the general curse
> Which twain have brought her to.

The Gentleman's words—supported by a whole network of relevant pointers—remain with us, and indeed only come into the fullness of their meaning as Cordelia is carried in, hanged. So do the themes of sacrifice and patience, with all their cosmic resonances. So does the destruction of the evil, and the destruction of evil within the soul: the category of rebirth. As, finally, Lear's heart breaks—almost as Gloucester's

> 'Twixt two extremes of passion, joy and grief,
> Burst smilingly—

we are confronted with a kind of 'My God, my God, why has thou forsaken me'. But, like that cry, this catastrophe has a context; and whatever its direct impact, it is only in its total context that it means what it means. In this context, even Lear's relapsing madness—apparently a final horror—may be madness only as this world goes. For the poetry has once more picked up the theme of blindness and seeing:

> Had I your tongues and eyes...
> Mine eyes are not of the best: I tell you straight.
> This is a dull sight.
> I'll see that straight.
> *Do you see this? Look on her, look, her lips,*
> *Look there, look there!*

Lear has come a long way. The world remains what it was, a merciless, heart-breaking world. Lear is broken by it, but he has learned to love and be loved; to gaze at the maddening cosmos through radical, 'foolish' love. Perhaps what he dies to see on Cordelia's lips may be no more illusory after all than what Leontes was to find on Hermione's. For Lear's experience can only lead either to *Timon* or to *The Winter's Tale*:

> we that are young
> Shall never see so much, nor live so long.

IV

Tragedy is a method of inquest into evil, and into the problem of evil. The question whether tragedy is compatible with the Christian religion is thus comparable to the question whether there can be a Christian philosophy. On the one hand, the search, in each case, must be free and self-determined; on the other hand, how can this autonomy be preserved within a context of faith?

We have seen Shakespeare's solution to this problem. Not that we should necessarily assume that he was writing from within a Christian commitment when he embarked on *Lear*. It is quite possible that he was not initially sure where his investigation was going to lead. In any case, nobody has ever accused him of loading his dice. Rejecting both his source play's Christian setting and happy ending and Holinshed's and Spenser's crucial accounts of *Cordelia's suicide*, Shakespeare shaped an image of human experience that has never been equalled in excruciating compulsion; and it is at the heart of *this* experience that we, so strangely, discover joy and peace. That joy is the joy of a saving truth about existence, or it is a cheat. We have no choice but to choose.

There is no report of this joy in accounts such as William Empson's or Jan Kott's. Indeed, Professor Kott, proposing a *Lear* à la Beckett, goes so far as to expurgate Cordelia from his reading—there is not a single reference to her in his essay—and then to sum up:

All bonds, all laws, whether divine, natural or human, are broken. Social order, from the kingdom to the family, will crumble into the dust. There are no longer kings and subjects, fathers and children, husbands and wives.[1]

Nevertheless, the play rests upon Cordelia's words:

> I love your majesty
> According to my bond; no more nor less

—and finally crowns its meanings with the incarnate measure of this nicety. And there are further prominent ranges of 'fact' directly contrary to Professor Kott's record. These were set out long ago by Bradley,[2] and there is no need to list them again here. But it is symptomatic that Kott's account of the disguised Edgar leading Gloucester to the imaginary precipice hardly registers that this happens to be a son—sinned against and intent on saving his father. (Before long, moreover, he is to figure as a subject mysteriously emerging to champion the king's

[1] *Shakespeare Our Contemporary*, p. 124.
[2] *Shakespearean Tragedy*, London, 1904; second edition, reprinted 1950, pp. 304–30.

cause, a reconciled brother—'Let's exchange charity'—
and a brokenly ennobled successor to the throne, still
obeying 'The weight of this sad time'.) Similarly, Professor Kott seems to find no problem in saying: 'There
are no longer kings and subjects, fathers and children,
husbands and wives'—and, on the next page: 'The banished Kent returns in disguise to his king.' Peter Brook's
production of *Lear* of 1962–3, inspired by Professor Kott's
essay, achieved its scrupulous fidelity to Beckettian aims
not only by a variety of theatrical skills, but by the excision
of Shakespearean impertinences like the two servants' tender comforting of the blinded Gloucester, or Edmund's
attempt to save Cordelia with his dying breath, and—it
being impossible to eliminate Cordelia in performance—
the cutting of the scene between Kent and the Gentleman
(IV, 3), in which her 'holy' and 'heavenly', richly creative
'passion'—'sunshine and rain at once'—is reported as
'like a better way'. The production even cut—surely
an ultimate in resolute emendation—the Gentleman's
epilogue following Lear's meeting with Gloucester in
mutually pitying impotence:

> Thou hast one daughter
> Who redeems nature from the general curse
> Which twain have brought her to.

Mr Brook can only have felt that these passages were
either too unimportant, or too important, to be retained.
His production was certainly an effective novelty. Its wide
international acclaim tells us much about contemporary
standards of literary and intellectual seriousness.

It may help to clarify the nature of the choice the play

so insistently imposes upon us to compare Professor Kott's view of Gloucester's suicide attempt with my own suggestions, above. Thus, for Professor Kott, Gloucester's prayer, as he prepares to kill himself, simply points to the metaphysical irrelevance of suicide in the world of the play:

> O you mighty gods!
> This world I do renounce, and, in your sights,
> Shake patiently my great affliction off:
> If I could bear it longer, and not fall
> To quarrel with your great opposeless wills,
> My snuff and loathed part of nature should
> Burn itself out. If Edgar live, O bless him!

This—and the 'parable' as a whole—is, for Professor Kott, merely 'cruel and mocking', like the end of *Waiting for Godot*:

> Gloster's suicide has a meaning only if the gods exist. It is a protest against undeserved suffering and the world's injustice. This protest is made in a definite direction. It refers to eschatology. Even if the gods are cruel, they must take this suicide into consideration. It will count in the final reckoning between gods and man. Its sole value lies in its reference to the absolute.
>
> But if the gods, and their moral order in the world, do not exist, Gloster's suicide does not solve or alter anything. It is only a somersault on an empty stage. It is deceptive and unsuccessful on the factual as well as on the metaphysical plane. Not only the pantomime, but the whole situation is then grotesque. From the beginning to the end. It is waiting for a Godot who does not come.

ESTRAGON. Why don't we hang ourselves?
VLADIMIR With what?
ESTRAGON You haven't got a bit of rope?

VLADIMIR No.

ESTRAGON Then we can't.

VLADIMIR Let's go.

ESTRAGON Wait, there's my belt.

VLADIMIR It's too short.

ESTRAGON You could hang on to my legs.

VLADIMIR And who'd hang on to mine?

ESTRAGON True.

VLADIMIR Show all the same. (*Estragon loosens the cord that holds up his trousers which, much too big for him, fall about the ankes. They look at the cord.*) It might do at a pinch. But is it strong enough?

ESTRAGON We'll soon see. Here.
    (*They each take an end of the cord and pull.*
    It breaks. They almost fall.)

VLADIMIR Not worth a curse.

(*Waiting for Godot*, II)

Gloster did fall, and he got up again. He has made his suicide attempt, but he failed to shake the world. Nothing has changed. Edgar's comment is ironical:

> ...had he been where he thought,
> By this had thought been past.
>
> (IV, 6)

If there are no gods, suicide is impossible. There is only death. Suicide cannot alter human fate, but only accelerate it. It ceases to be a protest and becomes the acceptance of the world's greatest cruelty—death. It is a surrender. Gloster has finally realized:

> ...henceforth I'll bear
> Affliction till it do cry out itself
> 'Enough, enough', and die.
>
> (IV, 6)[1]

Now I agree that there are real, significant relations between *King Lear* and Beckett (as there are between *Lear* and Chekhov). But it seems to me that Professor Kott's remarks on suicide make little contact with Beckett's text,

---

[1] Jan Kott, *Shakespeare our Contemporary*, pp. 120–2.

The Extreme Verge

and none at all with Shakespeare's. Kott's real attunement is surely with a third writer, who remains out of sight, though he is briefly mentioned later: Albert Camus. Isn't Professor Kott giving us a sort of transposed variation on *The Myth of Sisyphus*?

Camus surmounts suicide by deciding (i) that man's life consists of a necessary clash between reality and his absolute 'nostalgia for unity';[1] (ii) that, in this 'absurd' predicament, 'revolt gives life its value';[2] (iii) that 'revolt is the certainty of a crushing fate, without the resignation that ought to accompany it';[3] (iv) that 'suicide, like the leap, is acceptance at its extreme'.[4] (v) To 'leap' is to 'escape' or 'evade' absurd rational truth—a false commitment in virtue of which men 'deify what crushes them and find reason to hope in what impoverishes them'.[5] Religion is thus 'forced hope';[6] and suicide the ultimate sell-out: 'It is essential to die unreconciled and not of one's free will'.[7]

I think it could be shown that Camus's logic of revolt radically depends upon extra-logical decisions. Indeed, we could call it a forced desperateness. The philosophical rationale of this position does not directly concern us here. Its meaning for human living—and dying—is, however, most clearly brought to the test within literature. And here Shakespeare's 'ripeness' once more comes into its own. It is Gloucester's encounter with the abyss—his quasi-suicidal education for 'enoughness'—that reasons in

1 Albert Camus, *The Myth of Sisyphus*, London, 1955, p. 21.
2 *Ibid.*, p. 48.   3 *Ibid.*
4 *Ibid.*   5 *Ibid.*, p. 32.
6 *Ibid.*   7 *Ibid.*, p. 49.

our heart, as the 'opposeless' alternative to both suicide *and* any sort of 'unreconciled' self-condemnation to life.

Kott's talk of suicide as meanigful only as a 'protest against undeserved suffering and the world's injustice', and therefore as 'impossible'—a mere 'surrender'—'if there are no gods', is scarcely relevant even to *Waiting for Godot*. A whole complex of implications (which only a full analysis of Beckett's play as a whole could unravel) is active in the passage Kott quotes. But suicide as, conceivably, *protest* is not among them. Surges of 'protest' do indeed gather, break, re-form and break again throughout the play—as they do in *Lear*—but there is no suggestion in either play that this is what motivates suicide. Both in *Lear* and in *Waiting for Godot* suicide is simply the desire to quit—to

> Shake patiently my great affliction off

—or to 'go', once and for all, since every movement (or abstention from movement) is self-defeating. The passage quoted by Kott continues—in conclusion of what cannot be concluded:

(*Silence.*)

ESTRAGON You say we have to come back tomorrow?
VLADIMIR Yes.
ESTRAGON Then we can bring a good bit of rope.
VLADIMIR Yes.

(*Silence.*)

ESTRAGON Didi.
VLADIMIR Yes.
ESTRAGON I can't go on like this.
VLADIMIR That's what you think

ESTRAGON   If we parted? That might be better for us.

VLADIMIR   We'll hang ourselves tomorrow. (*Pause.*) Unless Godot comes.

ESTRAGON   And if he comes?

VLADIMIR   We'll be saved.

(*Vladimir takes off his hat (Lucky's) peers inside it, feels about inside it, shakes it, knocks on the crown, puts it on again.*)

ESTRAGON   Well? Shall we go?

VLADIMIR   Pull on your trousers.

ESTRAGON   What?

VLADIMIR   Pull on your trousers.

ESTRAGON   You want me to pull off my trousers?

VLADIMIR   Pull ON your trousers.

ESTRAGON   (*realizing his trousers are down.*) True.

　　　　　(*He pulls up his trousers. Silence.*)

VLADIMIR   Well? Shall we go?

ESTRAGON   Yes, let's go.

　　　　　(*They do not move.*)

CURTAIN

'Let's go. *They do not move*'; yet they 'can't go on like this'. They'll hang themselves 'tomorrow'. 'Unless Godot comes'. And tomorrow? Well, we know quite enough about that to be going on with. And yet—even now (even tomorrow, surely)—not enough to 'go'. It's not that suicide is discovered to fail as protest; it fails precisely as suicide. Suicide implies power: a residual control of one's destiny. But impotence, in this world, is total—and potently fated:

　　　—You could hang on to my legs.
　　　—And who'd hang on to mine?
　　　—True.

120

The Extreme Verge

Suicide implies real decision. But this presupposes a real, consummated, emancipation from all hope. And of course it implies extinction. But real, attainable nothingness assumes real knowledge (as Hamlet knew). Is it attainable even 'far away from here'—farther even than any of the emptinesses actually experienced within the play?:

ESTRAGON   Where shall we go?
VLADIMIR   Not far.
ESTRAGON   Oh, yes, let's go far away from here.
VLADIMIR   We can't.
ESTRAGON   Why not?
VLADIMIR   We have to come back tomorrow.
ESTRAGON   What for?
VLADIMIR   To wait for Godot.
ESTRAGON   Ah! (*Pause.*) He didn't come?
VLADIMIR   No.
ESTRAGON   And now it's too late.
VLADIMIR   Yes, now it's night.
ESTRAGON   And if we dropped him? (*Pause.*) If we dropped him.
VLADIMIR   He'd punish us. (*Silence. He looks at the tree.*) Everything's dead but the tree.[1]

Too late for Godot's coming, now that night is upon them (though it looks as though there'll be other days to come), it is still too soon to cease to fear him. It always will be. Especially in view of that tree:

ESTRAGON   (*looking at the tree*). What is it?
VLADIMIR   It's the tree.

[1] *Waiting for Godot*, p. 93. The passages quoted above follow on almost immediately.

ESTRAGON Yes, but what kind?

VLADIMIR I don't know. A willow.

> *Estragon draws Vladimir towards the tree. They stand motionless before it. Silence.*

It is this 'tree' upon which they would have to hang themselves—the same tree (or was it?) where we first found them at their 'appointment' (if that is what it was) with Godot (if that was his name); which later seems to have burst so mysteriously into leaf; and 'behind' which they have already so absurdly failed to 'disappear':

ESTRAGON I'm in hell!

VLADIMIR Where were you?

ESTRAGON They're coming there too!

VLADIMIR We're surrounded! (*Estragon rushes wildly towards back.*) Imbecile! There's no way out there

(as of course there cannot be, where hell is other people).

> There's no way out there. (*He takes Estragon by the arm and drags him towards the front. Gesture towards auditorium.*) There! Not a soul in sight! Off you go. Quick! (*He pushes Estragon towards auditorium. Estragon recoils in horror.*) You won't? (*He contemplates the auditorium.*) Well, I can understand that. Wait till I see. (*He reflects.*) Your only hope left is to disappear.

ESTRAGON Where?

VLADIMIR Behind the tree. (*Estragon hesitates.*) Quick! Behind the tree. (*Estragon goes and crouches behind the tree, realizes he remains in view, comes from behind the tree.*) Decidedly this tree will not have been of the slightest use to us.[1]

This tree they now contemplate, motionlessly, in silence: the tree of their hopes and despairs and perplexities and

---

[1] *Waiting for Godot*, p. 74.

terrors—Godot's tree, the life of their forced hope. In the end, we are left in all seriousness with the metaphysical question whether it is possible to 'disappear'—even by the use of suicide. In the world of *Waiting for Godot*—as in Gloucester's world—even the most elaborate suicide techniques are apt to be insufficient for disappearance. When the final curtain comes down, apparently merely repeating the paradox of trapped aspiration of the end of Act I

—Well? Shall we go?
—Yes, let's go.
(*They do not move.*)

—an intense, qualitative extension has thus been acted out, within the impotence to go and disappear, which finally precludes making an end of it all by disappearing.

There is, then, no question in *Waiting for Godot* of turning from suicide because this is useless as 'protest'—because it would mean 'acceptance' or 'surrender'. Indeed, its unwilled abandoning of an exit that may be no exit is itself an ultimate, trapped surrender. Gloucester's cliff bears even less relation to the proposition that 'if there are no gods, suicide is impossible'. Suicide is 'impossible' precisely in view of the gods. Mistakenly, Gloucester had claimed to 'Shake patiently my great affliction off': not as any sort of 'protest against undeserved suffering and the world's injustice', but, on the contrary—unable to 'bear it longer'—so as not to

fall
To quarrel with your great opposeless wills.

And it is to the gods that he re-dedicates himself in his

subsequent promise to bear affliction to the point of its consummation and self-release into death. This is why his escape from suicide—in 'free and patient' awaiting of his 'ripeness'—is, truly, an *escape*, and not merely a sentence of being trapped within his dark agony.[1] It is at once an agony of consummation and of rebirth. Henceforth his 'life's a miracle'. ' The fiend, the fiend', that 'led him to that place' was half tempter, half mask of filial—and cosmic—purpose. It is not long before we hear (though meanwhile Lear has met his 'child Cordelia' in his unbearable joy of reconciliation) that Gloucester at last knew Edgar as Edgar: ' 'Twixt two extremes of passion, joy and grief', his heart 'burst smilingly'. He saw him feelingly.

In Camus's terms, it could be objected that Gloucester, abetted by Edgar, 'deifies what crushes him and finds reason to hope in what impoverishes him'. And indeed, in a sense—turning Camus's inside out—this is exactly what happens. Utterly crushed and exposed, Gloucester finds reason to hope. This is the essential, secret rhythm of the whole play. Edgar and Kent are *both* right when, following Lear's dying words—'Look there, look there !'—they exclaim:

EDGAR   Look up, my Lord

(in what circumstances have we heard him say 'do but look up', before this?) and:

---

[1] Intermittent relapses, such as his 'No further, sir; a man may rot even here' (V, 2), merely measure the full, terrible distance of 'patience'. 'Ripeness is all'—so often quoted without reference to its context—is, essentially, a matter of 'enduring': far beyond the point where 'No further, sir' marks a 'rottenness' that short-circuits the destined consummation of a life-span.

KENT   Vex not his ghost: O! let him pass; he hates him
    That would upon the rack of this tough world
    Stretch him out longer.

Both responses are pertinent. Only a hair-breadth of darkness and silence divides Camus's commitment to 'metaphysical revolt' from Pascal's 'reasons of the heart'. Shakespeare takes us to 'the extreme verge', as Pascal does, and
ruthlessly insists that we distinguish and choose between
'forced hope' and the force of hope.

He does not by-pass our own choice. Nor could he
have done if he would, at the depth at which he is concerned to address us. It seems to me that this is where
H. A. Mason's complaints against *King Lear*[1] (and against
those who claim it as a central masterpiece) reveal a deep-
seated unsteadiness of focus. Following Middleton Murry,
he finds the play defective in unifying control, and com-
pares it unfavourably with *Macbeth*:

Is there any cause in Nature that makes these hard-hearts?
How much more interesting *King Lear* would be if Shakespeare could have answered this, his central question! We
have to wait for *Macbeth* to get any fresh insight. Here we are
merely presented with the facts.[2]

If I had to select 'the' question *King Lear* is most centrally asking, it would be 'What is the cause of thunder?',
rather than the more restricted, though obviously important, question Mr Mason picks out. But, be this as it
may, isn't the point, here, that *Macbeth* starts with *assuming*
that there is in fact *no* cause 'in nature' that could, by

[1] See his three articles in *The Cambridge Quarterly*, Winter 1966–7,
Spring 1967 and Summer 1967 (vol. II, nos. 1–3).
[2] *The Cambridge Quarterly*, vol. II, no. 2, pp. 160–1.

itself, account for the kind of evil it shows forth, just as 'nature' cannot of its own exorcise the 'supernatural' nightmare? It is these references—to a 'holy', as well as to a 'fiendish' transcendence—that *Lear* discovers, or rediscovers, within its dark seeing.

Not that incipient insight into 'the cause of thunder' means handing out 'answers' to the question posed by the storm (and the cliff, and the final deaths). To such questions there is, and can be, no 'answer' within the empirical world in which they are posed. What *King Lear* does, so starkly and 'so strangely', is to hint at another dimension of being, in which a final 'Look up, my Lord'—following 'look there, look there'!—is as pertinent to the final moments of heartbreak as 'O! let him pass'.

Mr Mason not only finds the end of the play 'significantly blank'—'Can we seriously maintain that it is as hopefully forward-looking as the end of *Macbeth*?'—but that 'the silence of all on stage when Lear dies should itself have sufficed to dismiss as an intrusive quirk of fancy that Lear dies of joy or bliss or in any way like Gloucester's death, as reported by Edgar'.[1] One can only repeat that such hope as there is in *Lear* is indeed *not* of the established, explicit character that *Macbeth* is to bring into play (precisely on the strength of concepts darkly and agonizingly struggling to birth, towards poetic availability, in *Lear*). As in Pascal's world,

All appearance indicates neither a total exclusion nor a manifest presence of divinity, but the presence of a God who hides Himself. Everything bears this character.[2]

---

[1] *The Cambridge Quarterly*, vol. II, no. 3, pp. 234–5.
[2] *Pensées*, p. 154, Everyman, London, 1931.

And though the play's end could, in this sense, be described as 'blank', how can Edgar's and Kent's sharply disjunctive responses be, jointly, described as 'silence'?

It is all the more remarkable that Mr Mason should fail to perceive this essentially non-assertive, and yet direction-forming, vision of *Lear* since he himself cites Pascal's *le coeur a ses raisons, que la raison ne connoist pas*—adding: 'and I do not suppose that Shakespeare would blush to have the phrase applied to his thinking'.[1] It is even more remarkable in view of the fact that Mr Mason is also concerned to show that it is the Gloucester plot that, at certain points, embodies 'the central stream' of the play. My own reading fully subscribes to this emphasis. Only, for Mr Mason, Gloucester's attempted suicide hardly makes sense:

Like a hero in a Greek Tragedy he knows he has reached a limit. He thinks the wrong he has done his son is irreparable. In the world of a Greek play his attempted suicide would be noble. What are we to make of it here? Is it a case of diabolic possession, and are we therefore glad to see him abused once again and once again the victim of a baby trick? Or if we take his resolution to be noble, is it not a pitiful come-down to find him so easily converted by Edgar? Can we see unambiguously what Shakespeare, what the play wants with Gloucester?[2]

Indeed, this is not a Greek tragedy. (Incidentally, one of the oddest persistent notions in criticisms of the play is that Edgar might be seen simply as a Stoic; as though we could by-pass the fact that for Stoicism suicide is a legitimate option.) For reasons we have looked into, heroic

[1] *The Cambridge Quarterly*, vol. II, no. 1, p. 39.
[2] *Ibid.*, vol. II, no. 3, p. 214.

limits and extreme 'baby tricks' are here indeed in intimate, searching interaction. And, for me, the analogy with Pascal's 'leap', from amidst his dizzying antinomies, makes good sense of the 'ambiguities' of Gloucester's experience—as of the play's experience as a whole. There is method in their elusiveness; they cumulatively build themselves into a complex, direction-revealing structure (though not if one treats Edgar as if he were mainly a realistic character—for whose 'cheap moralizing' one is 'longing for somebody to wring [his] neck').[1] It is in the Edgar–Gloucester scenes that the meaning not only of 'seeing' but of 'looking up'—beyond the play's still multiplying cliffs of fall—are acted out. Resonant with these hints, the deaths that conclude the play are empowered to evoke (though not to presume, or assert) an incipient eschatological perspective:

> Do you see this? Look on her, look, her lips,
> Look there, look there!

Lear's question challenges what *we* see—though this does not directly 'answer' his question about the thunder. And his dying imperatives (or exclamations) have the same sort of 'ambiguity' as the Gloucester scenes (though much less articulate in regard to these questions; it is simple facts that must now be allowed their say); and a similar doubleness resounds in Edgar's and Kent's responses. We are required to 'look at *her*'—the sheer, irreducible temporal violation. But, equally, we are to look, as Lear himself did, in ultimate concentration, on 'her *lips*' ('Lend me a looking-glass; / If that her breath will mist or stain the

[1] *The Cambridge Quarterly*, vol. II, no. 3, pp. 230–1.

128

stone, / Why then she lives'). Edgar's 'Look up, my Lord' completes the play's massively intricate weaving of pointers to 'seeing' and 'looking'. Fleeting and off-hand as this final, reminding pointer must be here, so as not to pre-judge or disown the bare, insupportable perceptions that this work needs to leave us with, it nevertheless leaves us with resonances not simply reducible to 'the rack of this tough world'.

The most subtle formulation known to me of the view that *King Lear* is a tragedy in which 'all moral structures, whether of natural order or Christian redemption, are invalidated by the naked fact of experience', is Nicholas Brooke's *Shakespeare: King Lear*.[1] Professor Brooke responds so finely to the play's idiom, and has such a firm grip upon its problems that disagreement with his conclusions can largely be based on evidences he himself helps to bring into view. Thus, he recognizes 'Dover' as 'an emblem of renewal, towards which everyone moves as towards the light at the end of the tunnel'. Through it, 'a regenerative movement is set going (developing from Kent's soliloquy in II, 2) before the storm reaches its full violence. That violence will not, we are assured, be the play's final comment; an impulse towards tragi-comedy (implying a happy ending) is felt already here, and it will grow strongly in Act IV.'[2] But while Professor Brooke fully accepts the mock-suicide scene as a 'moral exemplum'[3] or 'moral allegory'[4] in which Edgar's

[1] Nicholas Brooke, *Shakespeare: King Lear*, London, 1963, pp. 59–60.
[2] *Ibid.*, p. 32.　　　　[3] *Ibid.*, p. 38.
[4] *Ibid.*, p. 43.

Think that the clearest gods, who make them honours
Of men's impossibilities, have preserved thee

'is a distinct affirmation', 'impressively' acknowledged
by Gloucester,[1] he sees the Gloucester plot as ultimately
'almost a kind of irony':[2] 'that Gloucester's despair can
be relieved only makes it plainer that Lear's cannot'.[3]
Similarly, Professor Brooke recognizes the Gentleman's
words of Act IV, Scene 6,
>   Thou hast one daughter
> Who redeems nature from the general curse
> Which twain have brought her to

as implying Adam and Eve, as well as Regan and Goneril,
and so as evoking 'the Christian redemption of the general
curse on nature';[4] and he accepts that Lear 'dies believing
Cordelia to be alive';[5] but this seems to him merely (as
it did to Professor Empson)[6] a final, desolating relapse
into delusion.[7] 'What we *feel* is finally justified against
all the moral impulsions of what we "ought" to say'.[8]
There is no reason why tragedy should not leave us depressed. 'It is the business of a tragedy, of the play itself,
to be depressing; if in the end it is really encouraging,
the sense of disaster will be contained, and the demands on
our feelings less acute'.[9]

The process of the play seems to me calculated to repudiate
every source of consolation with which we might greet the
final disaster. Not even the most perfunctory of reassurances

---

[1] Brooke, *Shakespeare: King Lear*, p. 43.   [2] *Ibid.*, p. 39.
[3] *Ibid.*   [4] *Ibid.*, p. 45.
[5] *Ibid.*, p. 55.   [6] Cf. p. 111 above.
[7] Brooke, *Shakespeare: King Lear*, pp. 53–5
[8] *Ibid.*, p. 55.   [9] *Ibid.*, p. 56.

is uttered after Lear has died, and we must assent to Kent's words:

> O! let him pass; he hates him
> That would upon the rack of this tough world
> Stretch him out longer. (V, 3, 313–15)

If that is our final sense of the play, we cannot honestly point to anything that has gone before it as a source of comfort.[1]

Professor Brooke's argument cannot be adequately represented in this summary form; I hope that the reader will wish to re-examine it in full. But I believe that it is not to disown, or underestimate, the force of his account to reaffirm my own 'sense of the play' in face of his emphases.

Once more, it is the Pascal analogy I should like to start with. If *Lear* is indeed, like the *Pensées*, an exposure in depth of radical antinomies—pointing to faith (faith—not 'geometric' demonstration) then we would not expect its catastrophe to be other than catastrophic, we would not expect 'consolation' to be held out to us on a plate before we go home. What we might expect, if such an inquest is indeed at work here, is: (i) a full evocation of *both* sides of the engulfing clash; (ii) a ripening presence of potentially sufficient epiphanies of redemption; and (iii) a resolutely guarded insistence on the tragic thing itself—which, empirically, must remain what it was. All these, it seems to me, in fact feature in the play—and Professor Brooke comes extremely close to acknowledging them all. How, then, do the ultimate, infinite divergencies in our interpretations arise?

The nearest one can get to identifying the nature of these differences is in terms of (ii). Clearly, for Professor

---

[1] *Ibid.*, p. 57.

Brooke the 'redemptive' significances within the play are
not 'sufficient'—and he might therefore have difficulty in
understanding what exactly could be meant by calling
them even '*potentially* sufficient epiphanies'. And yet he
himself largely devotes his own analysis to confronting
the challenge of images of 'renewal', of 'regeneration',
of religious 'affirmation'—indeed, even one evoking 'the
Christian redemption of the general curse on nature'. At
the least, these evocations are 'potentially sufficient' in the
tautological, though surely not trivial, sense that for some
qualified readers or hearers they in fact turn out to be
sufficient. In a maximum sense, their 'potential sufficiency'
could consist in being designed to show forth significances
whose real contextual bearings of their nature easily elude
perception. ('The prophecies, the very miracles and proofs
of our religion', says Pascal, 'are not of such a nature that
they can be said to be absolutely convincing. But they
are also of such a kind that it cannot be said that it is
unreasonable to believe them. Thus there is both evidence
and obscurity to enlighten some and confuse others. But
the evidence is such that it surpasses, or at least equals,
the evidence to the contrary; so that it is not reason which
can determine men not to follow it...').[1] And do not
critics concerned to weigh the 'evidences' of the play
in regard to these questions acknowledge by this very concern that redemptive significances might really be 'sufficient' within it—despite all that might take it totally
beyond 'consolation' or 'comfort'? Critics do not, after
all, expend labour disputing such questions as whether

[1] *Pensées*, p. 156.

Goneril is, or is not, an admirable daughter, whether Iago is truly Othello's moral peer, or whether there is, or there is not, a real renewal of the 'sickly weal' of Scotland at the end of *Macbeth*. They are, however, quite properly concerned to ask whether the Fool or Edgar—or, for that matter, Iago—function essentially as 'realistic' characters; whether Othello's tragedy really has its source in loving 'not wisely but too well'; or whether the images of religious 'affirmation' in *King Lear* survive, or fail to survive, as positive presences within our 'final sense of the play'. It is a common fact of literary interpretation that some of our most vital decisions often have to emerge from complex—and even perhaps, apparently contradictory—evidences. If these decisions are not to be arbitrary, some of these evidences must be 'potentially sufficient'—in the maximum sense. What is the nature of these suasions in *King Lear*?

The clashes of evidence in *Lear* are more central, more drastic, more dynamically stable, than in any other complex of meanings in Shakespeare. This is of the essence of what it would have us see—and see by. To some readers, like Mr Mason, these clashes in fact seem so sovereign as to make for 'radical incoherence'. To others, they do not pose any special problems at all. Thus, for Professor Kott and Mr Peter Brook *Lear* hardly even raises the question whether our 'final sense of the play' should include elements of 'affirmation': anything smacking of affirmation is instantly and confidently banished from the whole drama. Professor Brooke resists both these courses. To him the play holds together alright. And it must hold without reductive simplification. Giving full weight to those elements in the play which might at any rate *seem* to point towards 'renewal' or 'redemption', he cannot but be aware that there will be according resonances that must be absorbed into one's 'final sense of the play', that cannot be simply displaced by the final simplicities of the 'rack'.

Nevertheless, in the last resort Professor Brooke seems to me to parallel the Kott–Brooke *reductio*. Simply to say that 'the final sense is that all moral structures, whether of natural order or Christian redemption are invalidated by the naked fact of experience' simply disowns the poetic complexities that both create and define this 'fact'. The devastation we end with grows out of the cumulative significances we have been through. It does not cancel, or supersede them. It is entirely of a piece with the tragic logic that presses towards these ultimacies. In this sense, these 'facts' are as complex as they are simple—as definitively 'accommodated' as they are naked. Fusing these ultimate 'facts' with its whole cumulative structure of seeing, the play leaves no room for any sort of emotional positivism. Conceivably, its conclusion might torture preceding redemptive annunciations into ironies; but then the effect could only be a proportionate, nihilistic grotesqueness—redemptive annunciations killed for sport. What it cannot conceivably do is to 'invalidate' these annunciations by way of cancelling them; it cannot leave us in simple, naked proximity to 'the facts'. Had Shakespeare chosen to do without such emphases as the Gloucester–Edgar scenes, the insistent tragic probing of 'blindness' and 'seeing', the timeless moment, in IV, 7, of Lear's renewed relation to Cordelia, and Cordelia's association with 'the Christian redemption of the general curse on nature',[1] a simple immediate response to the 'facts' would suffice. Given these emphases, however, such an empiricism is the one option the play disqualifies out of hand. Its 'facts'—it insists—inhere within a dimension beyond mortal limits. If the tragedy is coherent, this coherence can only be metaphysical: either relating to an ultimate hope beyond 'the rack'; or to an ultimate metaphysical outrage. The alternatives may be set out schematically:

1. 'Salvation' and 'redemption' remain valid 'affirmations' within the play's total structure.

2. 'Salvation' and 'redemption' are not only invalidated, but revealed as diabolically refined cultivations of human illusion.

3. Ultimately there is no unifying structure at all.

What is 'sufficiently' precluded by the terms of the play is:

4. A unifying structure, 'invalidating' religious affirmations, which leaves us merely with secular meanings. ('Large orders collapse; but values remain, and are independent of them'.[2])

In practice, of course, a critic's conclusions may not be so clean-cut. Mr Mason tends towards (3). Professor Brooke, wishing to assert (4), in effect seems to hover between (2) and (3). In so far as he acknowledges apparent religious 'affirmations' within the play, but regards these

[1] Brooke, *Shakespeare: King Lear*, p. 45 (cf. p. 130 above).
[2] Brooke, *Shakespeare: King Lear*, p. 60.

as ultimately rendered 'ironic' by the 'facts', he must tend towards (2). For why, for instance, should Shakespeare subject Gloucester to all this Dover symbolism if he were ultimately concerned to show that supernatural meanings are merely *irrelevant*? Gloucester can only be seen as either in the hands of purposeful salvific powers, or as gratuitously pushed around by no less purposeful 'wanton boys'. The one way we cannot see him is in a common-sense 'factual' perspective. His elaborate processing into an 'endurance' beyond all limits is either a real *divina commedia* or an obscene daemonic farce. This is the depth at which any decision that 'all moral structures, whether of natural order or Christian redemption, are invalidated by the naked facts of experience' would have to operate in this play. But Professor Brooke does not really wish to hold that the play is a metaphysical farce, or a tragedy of cosmic outrage. He merely offers to *neutralize* its *prima facie* religious 'affirmations'. And this, I suggest, is just what cannot be done without, in effect, writing off the play's claim to serious poetic coherence. If its theological probings, at 'the extreme verge', are serious, it cannot go on to cut loose from this whole theological dimension as the final 'facts' close in; not without disintegrating as a total poetic image. So it is that Professor Brooke, despite his manifest concern for the integrity of the text, almost arrives at a Kott–Brook emphasis (indeed, he is able to speak of Peter Brook's 'justly celebrated...production' of the play[1]), qualified by the admission of meanings which can hardly be shown to cohere with such a structure.

[1] Brooke, *Shakespeare, King Lear*, p. 28 (footnote).

It seems to me that Professor Brooke holds the key to the Dover sequence in speaking of it as virtual 'tragi-comedy' inserted within a tragic action:

Edgar and Gloucester give us what the play would be, if it were a moralising tragi-comedy (when Shakespeare does write such a play, *The Winter's Tale*, he does it far more persuasively); the contrast between sub-plot and main plot here is one of genre as well as depth.[1]

But to what purpose does Shakespeare thus seem to mingle his genres? What is it he here wishes to be 'persuasive' about? Is he really just concerned to contrast the 'depth' of the two tragic predicaments, 'so that all the argument has a double value, almost a kind of irony: it means one thing about Gloucester, but another about Lear'?[2] ('And Edgar's moral tone, offered as comfort to the one, seems, in relation to the other, harsh and false'.[3])

It certainly would not do if 'Edgar' were made to change places with 'Cordelia' within the two plots—though both push their fathers beyond endurance: whether by being what they are, or by ceasing to be; whether as bringing to ripeness a virtually posthumous enduring, or by actually releasing life, through death. These significances indeed have a 'double value'; but their relation is hardly 'ironic'. The relation is not expressible in terms of relative 'depth' at all. (To express the relation in terms of such ironies would indeed imply an ultimate grotesqueness, would reduce *both* experiences to absurdity—in a Beckett or Kott-Brook sense.) The point is precisely that any potential 'irony' on these lines is disqualified, or trans-

[1] *Ibid.*, p. 38.   [2] *Ibid.*, p. 39.   [3] *Ibid.*

cended. It is transcended since, in this context, the word 'depth' (or any equivalent term) is rendered radically ambiguous. For in *both* plots we have to ask: is the deepest reality a matter of fact—or a fact of 'riper' seeing? This is the handy-dandy on which *Lear* centrally turns. Thunder, madness, blindness and heart-break—all demand a choice between depth and depth of response. What else could the elements of 'tragi-comedy' à la *The Winter's Tale* be doing within the 'factual' depths of *Lear*? Will not *The Winter's Tale* and *The Tempest* have consummate depths of their own—though (for this very purpose) distanced, by poetic convention, from the full depth of those 'facts' that *Lear* must first show forth in their own blinding, maddening bareness?

For *The Winter's Tale* only the final seeing finally matters. In *King Lear*, 'seeing' and 'feeling'—in the immediate here and now—are tragically complementary. Neither 'seeing' nor 'feeling' exceeds the other in their final claims upon us; neither displaces, or depreciates, the other. It really matters that Lear dies—and dies the way he dies. It matters that Cordelia dies. To say to him, as Cleomenes is to say to Leontes (*W.T.*, V, 1):

> Sir, you have done enough, and have perform'd
> A saint-like sorrow: no fault could you make
> Which you have not redeem'd; indeed, paid down
> More penitence than done trespass—

or to declare, as Paulina is to declare (*W.T.*, V, 3):

> That she is living,
> Were it but told you, should be hooted at
> Like an old tale: but it appears she lives,
> Though yet she speaks not—

would be grotesquely out of place. Equally, however, it matters that 'tragi-comic' significances are, nevertheless, an integral part of the tragedy—both as echoing within the catastrophic conclusion and as themselves completed, and consummated, by these ultimate matters of fact. In the end, the choice apparently exacted from us—between 'tragic' and 'tragi-comic' significances, between 'feeling' and 'seeing'—is revealed as merely provisional. Finally it is not a matter of *either/or* but of *both/and*. Lear's experience insists on the absoluteness of temporal facts. But we cannot therefore conclude that 'Edgar's morality play is exposed by Lear's experience'.[1] The Gloucester plot is not simply Edgar's; nor does it simply moralize. It has genuine tragic depths of its own. It cannot be hooted, or wept, out of Lear's universe.

Shakespearean romance or 'tragi-comedy' of the type foreshadowed within *Lear* is, as modern criticism has shown, anything but a doctoring of tragic experience in the interests of a holiday from life, or of *a priori* edification. It is, rather, a process of *assimilating* the meaning of tragic experience itself, by a poetic discipline involving a considerable degree of abstraction, with the consequent freedom to allow tragic 'facts' to try on the clothes of received conceptual forms—themselves poetically recreated in the process. That Shakespeare chose to employ, for these purposes, some rather tall stories in danger of being 'hooted at like an old tale' does not compromise their serious suitability for his ends. And would it not be odd if, towards the end of his life, Shakespeare had thus

[1] Brooke, *Shakespeare: King Lear*, p. 59.

come to employ, systematically, a poetic idiom already '*exposed* by Lear's experience'? And odd to the point of incredibility, that he should actually elaborate in these works the very conceptual garments 'exposed' by that experience?

The rationale of *The Winter's Tale* and *The Tempest* is to investigate processes beyond the limits of profane possibility. In these works, tragic facts are exhibited within poetic-conceptual structures in which time is not only shown as directed towards eternity, but as itself potentially open to eternal marvels of renewal and transformation. Time and eternity enter into each other. So inextricable is their relation that their action upon, and their mirroring of, each other, often approaches a many-levelled poetic continuum. Temporally irremediable estrangements and losses are subject to rebirths beyond all drowning. Hermione's motionless image—'What was he that did make it?' (V, 3, 63)—re-enters as breathing life. But not before Leontes is bidden:

> No longer shall you gaze on't, lest your fancy
> May think anon it moves (V, 3, 60–61)—

and confesses:

> No settled senses of the world can match
> The pleasure of that madness (V, 3, 72–3).

Could Shakespeare here, without knowing what he is doing, be collapsing into fancies and pleasures precisely such as were 'exposed' as simple tragic illusions by *Lear*? Or is he deliberately replaying his own deepest tragic recognitions in order to disown them? Or is he perhaps

merely pot-boiling, in frivolous self-exploitation and detachment from his own art?

The alternative is to recognize an authentic continuity
between illusion and reality in *King Lear* and illusion and
reality in Shakespeare's last plays. It is, after all, beyond
question that one of the central concerns of *Lear* is with
the break-down of common-sense realism—a simultaneous
transcendence of common-sense categories on the level of
poetic-dramatic technique, and on that of tragic 'seeing'.
Though there is a sense in which Gloucester's experience
forms a special 'exemplum' within the play, and I have
so far accepted Professor Brooke's ambiguous 'tragi-
comic' label for it, it is time to stress the complementary
truth—that the Gloucester plot is thoroughly at home
within the tragedy's total idiom and poetic logic.

It is not necessary to catalogue the ways in which *King
Lear*—from the division of the kingdom, to the storm and
final combat—pushes beyond the limits of realism and
common-sense 'facts'. But, although Professor Brooke is
well aware of this drive towards 'a pattern, a significance'
—by methods approaching 'allegory'—all this, to him,
merely gives shape to impulses which the play exists to
frustrate and silence:

The final sense is that all moral structures, whether of
natural order or Christian redemption, are invalidated by the
naked fact of experience. The dramatic force of this rests on
the impulse to discover a pattern, a significance, by in-
vestigating nature. But nature itself finally frustrates that
impulse; when Lear dies, the moral voices are silenced.[1]

[1] Brooke, *Shakespeare: King Lear*, pp. 59–60.

To which one can only reply: 'voices', yes, *seeing*, no.
We are still required to 'look'—and to 'look up'. To
register the voices as 'silenced' without continuing to
look at the 'facts' through the symbolic structures that
create, and sustain them, and actually hold them up to
us, could only be consistent with a play that finally falls
to pieces.

Thus, Professor Brooke recognizes that Lear's scenes
are not, when all has been said, really 'so widely different'
from the 'obviously allegorical' scenes between Edgar and
Gloucester in the last two Acts. But while 'the moral
demonstration' in the Gloucester scenes 'continually exceeds the dramatic experience, or at least is disproportionately obtrusive', Lear's experience leaves us 'profoundly
moved'.[1]

Yet Lear's scenes are not so widely different: Lear waking in
Cordelia's arms, or Cordelia dead in Lear's arms likwise have
allegorical significance (I have remarked how often the stage
picture is emblematic). The difference between these two is
not fortuitous: Edgar's morality play is exposed by Lear's
experience; or by contrary, we are assured of the naturalness
of Lear's experience partly by feeling its contrast with the
demonstrative allegory applied to Gloucester. The sense of
'naturalness' in drama is always partly relative; if one scene
is more natural than its predecessor, we may easily come to feel
that it is absolutely natural.[2]

But this apparently 'absolutely natural' experience that
is itself 'emblematic'—is emblematic of what? For Professor Brooke it can only be an emblem 'exposing'
Edgar's 'morality play'—an allegory casting out allegory.

[1] Brooke, *Shakespeare, King Lear*, p. 59.   [2] *Ibid.*

But, apart from the oddity of such an ambition, especially in such a play (it has, one would have thought, enough work on its hands to dispense with such esoteric lit. crit. business), such a self-cannibalistic form could not digest what it would devour. To see the final facts as rivalling and disowning—rather than as fulfilling—the structuring significances of the advancing drama is to dismember the entire defining structure. For how would such an 'invalidating' of 'all moral structures, whether of natural order or Christian redemption' leave such significances (significantly independent of 'Edgar's morality play') as the Gentleman's comment relating Cordelia to 'the Christian redemption of the general curse on nature'?[1]

> Thou hast one daughter,
> Who redeems nature from the general curse
> Which twain have brought her to.

Do these chorically challenging, calmly amazing—almost oracular—words, and all the related poetic evocations concerning Cordelia, form a further 'disproportionately obtrusive' pattern, simply brought in so as to be *'silenced'* by the end of the play? Or are we just meant to *forget* them, as Mr Peter Brook actually cut them from his production? Perhaps the most significant silence, here, is Professor Brooke's own; he has very little to say about the relation between Cordelia as an 'emblem' of Christian redemption and 'Edgar's morality play'; and nothing at all about how these 'allegorical' hints of redemption surrounding Cordelia might bear upon the 'absolutely natural' 'allegory' of Cordelia dead in Lear's arms. He

---

[1] *Ibid.*, p. 45 (cf. pp. 130 and 134–5 above).

merely finds that, when Lear 'retreats into a sympathetic delusion' because the 'barren truth is unbearable'—

> This feather stirs; she lives! If it be so,
> It is a chance which does redeem all sorrows
> That ever I have felt—

'It is not so; and nothing is redeemed'.[1] But the classic emblem of Christian redemption is itself an unstirring, executed body. And the question one cannot help asking here is why Shakespeare should choose to recall, at this 'allegorical' climax of 'natural experience', the 'allegory' of Christian redemption so extraordinarily built into the pagan experience of the play (just as Lear and Edgar, between them, reactivate those 'allegorical' diagnoses of 'looking' and 'looking up' that should at any rate challenge our empiricist confidence in 'absolutely natural' modes of perception). If 'nothing is redeemed'—despite the transcendent perspectives the play insists on—Cordelia could only lie before us as an ultimate epiphany of cosmic 'sport': an emblem not merely of unbearable human loss, but of *fulfilment*: of 'wanton' annunciations of redemption. In such perspectives, that she is living, were it but told us, should be hooted at like an old tale. But we are in the world of post-mediaeval tragedy; not that of Beckettian farce. Though the pleasure of that madness—'look on her, look, her *lips*'—belongs here more directly to madness proper than to the gaze of faith, it has behind it more penitence than done trespass, and a deeply 'enduring' discipline of seeing feelingly. It would be surprising if Samuel Beckett were one day to give us a sort of *Winter's Tale* (though

[1] Brooke, *Shakespeare: King Lear*, pp. 53–4.

much more surprising were he simply to turn to 'absolutely natural' records of experience). It is not at all surprising that *The Winter's Tale* should follow *King Lear*.

If it is asked, 'But surely you cannot mean that Cordelia, however saintly, is to be equated with Christ, or to be actually held to "redeem"?', my reply would be twofold. First, if there is here, and in Cordelia's treatment as a whole, a re-enactment of Christ's sacrificial drama, this need not at all imply any sort of personal or metaphysical *equation*. The immediate meaning is simply that Cordelia's life and death fall within a significatory pattern —*incomplete at the point where the play ends* (*the point where common sense ends*)—defined by the Gospels—and whose completion lies beyond common sense. For those who now cannot assent to 'news' of resurrection (whether Christ's own, or a general resurrection at the end of time) the emblem of the man on a cross must tend to be simply an emblem of death—though a death beginning, as well as ending, an illusion. For Shakespeare's contemporaries, however, the love-death recalled by the cross was still culturally alive with the concepts of resurrection and eternal life. However the emphases of the Christian imagination may have shifted over the centuries—and specifically in face of the challenges of the Renaissance— the cross as a living emblem could never be merely a record of a mere catastrophic 'fact'.

But, secondly, the 'emblematic' conclusion of *Lear* not only *evokes* the Gospel passion redeeming

> nature from the general curse
> Which twain have brought her to.

It could quite properly suggest an actual *participation* in this passion—and action, as St Paul speaks of completing in his flesh 'what is lacking in Christ's afflictions' (Col. i, 24). The mystery of vicarious suffering, and the potentiality of ordinary human suffering to be taken up into the central Christian action, is especially manifest in the saint, though it underlies the whole imperative hope of 'redeeming the time'. (This is the central theme of *Murder in the Cathedral*, with its recurrent emphasis 'that action is suffering / And suffering is action'—indeed, it underlies all Eliot's later work; the theme is similarly central to G. M. Hopkins.) Within the pre-Christian framework of *Lear*—ensuring a sharply renewed response to the natural mysteries upon which the Christian mystery is grafted— these significances can only be 'hints and guesses / Hints followed by guesses'; but is there not an incipiently intelligible connection between the scenes of Lear's reunion with Cordelia (and Gloucester's with Edgar) and the 'wheel of fire' that consumes their life? Within the tragic world of this 'wheel', Cordelia—the 'soul in bliss' whom Lear addresses, awaking in wonder, as if from another world (IV, 7)—has yet to complete her final tragic revolution upon the wheel; and so has Lear himself. Vicarious suffering—

> For thee oppressed king, am I cast down;
> Myself could else out-frown false Fortune's frown
>
> (V, 3, 5)

and the guilt-conscious ecstasy of Lear's 'If you have poison for me, I will drink it' (IV, 7, 72) are united upon a single, redemptive wheel. In this sense—though of course one could not possibly 'wish' that it should come to this—even the ultimate racked howls of the final dereliction can be (just) glimpsed as consummating this unity. And does not the fragile, equivocal, poignant, almost insupportable joy of Lear's awaking—

You do me wrong to take me out of the grave—

darkly prefigure the timeless resurrected relations of the end of the *Winter's Tale* and *Tempest*—as well as resounding, with latent *cathartic* power, within the consummate tragic facts of the end of *King Lear* itself?

Shakespeare was well aware that tragedy must be fully tragic; not only to come into its own, but, equally, if it is to provide proportionate soil for news of resurrection. It is not yet time for his parables of eternity. *Lear* is the moment of break-through.[1] There is nothing that could take its place. Here, Shakespeare sets out the alternatives, in terms which—if we can let them do it—can probe our hearts to the root. Where the purpose is to leap from seeing to seeing, we can only be addressed feelingly, in darkness. In *Lear* this darkness is 'riper', more absolute in its probing, than *Three Sisters* of why 'We must go on living, we must'; of why thoughts of 'No further, sir' are 'ill'; why of

Men must endure
Their going hence, even as their coming hither.

[1] Cf. L. C. Knights's important essay in *Some Shakespearean Themes*, London, 1959: 'What our seeing has been directed towards is nothing less than *what man is*' (original italics, p. 117). 'For what takes place in *King Lear* we can find no other word than renewal' (p. 119).

It is more intensely searching, and more deeply revealing within its 'enduring', than the 'absurd' immobility of *Waiting for Godot*. It takes us, it seems to me, into a more securely poised humanism than Camus's. Which, after all, is the more open to absolute truth (an absoluteness that, as Camus himself stresses, is necessarily beyond human limits): an 'unlimited campaign against the heavens for the purpose of capturing a king who will first be dethroned and finally condemned to death';[1] or a tragic learning that moves from confident outrage—

> But yet I call you servile ministers,
> That have with two pernicious daughters join'd
> Your high-engendered battles 'gainst a head
> So old and white as this. O! O! 'tis foul—

to
> I am mainly ignorant
> What place this is, and all the skill I have
> Remembers not these garments—?

Which is the more absolute for human transformation (though Camus's hunger for justice and brotherhood is beyond doubt): a chronic 'revolt' without hope of redemption; or the struggling perception, within methodical despair:
> Thou hast one daughter,
> Who redeems nature from the general curse
> Which twain have brought her to—?

Which, indeed, is the more simply humane: a denial of suicidal release in the interests of dying 'unreconciled and not of one's free will';[2] or an imperative—both beyond stoicism, and beyond 'revolt'—

---

[1] Albert Camus, *The Rebel*, London, 1954, p. 31.
[2] Cf. p. 118 above.

—No further, sir; a man may rot even here.
—What! in ill thoughts again? Men must endure
  Their going hence, even as their coming hither:
  Ripeness is all. Come on—

pointing to a harvest beyond all rotting?

V

Shakespeare's use of the tragic medium is as various as
the stages of his artistic growth. It can be purely descriptive—as in some of the history plays—with no general
tragic world-picture implied. It can be drily diagnostic,
as in *Othello*, or frantically nihilistic, as in *Timon of Athens*.
In *Hamlet* we seem to have an endeavour to work towards
a tragic resolution, though not wholly matured; for while
such a resolution is clearly implicit in the play's general
drift, and approaches realization at many points, we remain too much in the world of *Troilus* to be carried into
the fullness of tragic peace. (It is its objective, well-
fermented pessimism that renders *Othello*, the later play,
so clear-edged and lucid in contrast.)

King *Lear* is the pivot of Shakespeare's entire career.
What it succeeds in re-stating—with supreme urgency and
completeness—and at the same time resolving, from within the depths of that statement itself, took the whole of
his preceding experience to mature; and what follows is
wholly the fruit of this achievement. In *Macbeth*, evil—the
evil of the problem plays, of *Hamlet* and of *Othello*—is
simultaneously available from within and from without;
as a psychological fact, that convicts us of complicity, and
as a spiritual fact objectified for our contemplation. What

could previously be united only in flashes—since one cannot both live through and comprehend an *obsession*—is at last realized in a unity of exorcizing penetration. Evil can now be come to terms with, because 'the problem of evil'—the cosmic mystery—has been come to terms with. What *Lear* discovers, *Macbeth* assumes: *Macbeth* is a fully explicit Christian image. Its *catharsis* is brought about by a three-fold epiphany: the showing forth of the essential foreignness of evil in the world it infests—with a complementary rediscovery of the great 'natural' values ('As honour, love, obedience, troops of friends') violated and forfeited by the evil-doers; an epiphany of the divine presence within and above this natural order, manifesting its absolute, redemptive power; and a compassionate, 'costing' assimilation of the mystery of damnation. It is as if *Hamlet* had re-emerged, with Claudius at the dramatic centre, and as if Hamlet–Macduff, at last an unperplexed instrument of Providence, need no longer make mouths at Fortinbras. If *Macbeth* thus completes the religious transcendence of evil, *Antony and Cleopatra* confirms the validity of wordly goodnesses as such. *Antony and Cleopatra*—like *Coriolanus*—is scrupulously naturalistic: *King Lear* and *Macbeth* have done their job, and it only remains frontally to reaffirm what in these works could only be secondary—the 'bounty' and 'rareness' of the world itself, for all its failings and falsehoods. With Cordelia in the background, even erotic love has come full circle: Cressida is redeemed in Cleopatra. And so, everything is ready for the final plays, in which tragedy is recollected in tranquillity and Shakespeare writes his own commentaries on what has gone before. These commentaries once more tell of a world in travail, but conventionally distance its evil, so that both its redemption within time and the 'heavenly music' beyond shall be finally explicit:

> It is requir'd
> You do awake your faith...
>
> Music, awake her: strike! (*Music*)
> 'Tis time; descend; be stone no more; approach;
> Strike all that look upon with marvel. Come;
> I'll fill your grave up: stir; nay, come away;
> Bequeath to death your numbness, for from him
> Dear life redeems you. (*W.T.*, V, 3.)

To say that tragedy is incompatible with faith is not to take the measure of Shakespeare: it is either to trivialize him or to disown him. Tragedy, in its fullness, starts from the fact of Cordelia's death, and in a sense ends there. And yet, only just audibly, it hints: 'All shall be well and all manner of thing shall be well'. If it starts anywhere else, it fails to present the full tragic problem; if it ends with less, it is less a tragedy than an outcry—though there are contexts in which we shall always want to go on talking about *Lear* and *Ghosts* under the same general heading.

Tragedy, fully ripened, says: 'nevertheless'; and, at its greatest: 'even because'. It is never betrayed into a glib 'never mind', or a purely desperate 'see!' or 'it doesn't matter'. It may include gestures of ultimate despair or revolt, and may even place these—as *Lear* does—at its very centre of vision; but it also possesses a point of rest, where a costly peace is maturing.

On a cosmic plane—wherever, that is, tragedy raises the most ultimate questions of all—such a *catharsis* can only be religious. For either there is a meaning beyond the merely human, or there is only the terrible fact. Cosmic tragedy at its greatest—involving some kind of ultimate 'reconciliation'—is therefore always religious—whether in Aeschylus or Sophocles or Shakespeare.

Where no such reconciliation emerges, or where the tragic problem is limited to areas not raising these ultimate questions at all, tragic *catharsis*—of a more limited sort—is still possible in terms of heroic sublimity, vindicating human greatness, and particular values like courage, loyalty and love. Of this, the greatest example in literature is *Antony and Cleopatra*.

Where, however, there is no cosmic reconciliation, nor any sort of heroic transcendence, only the tragic *problem* remains, and we are left with what, from one point of view, may still be called tragedy, but what—in its failure to reconcile, or resolve, or release—is, from another point of view, the *failure* of tragic power.

That is why the modern world is increasingly devoid of tragic resources. It is neither in vital contact with what Shakespeare points to in *King Lear*, nor any longer so sure that Antony and Cleopatra are the mould in which humankind is made:

TUZENBAKH Forget your two or three hundred years, because even in a million years life will still be just the same as ever. It doesn't change, it always goes on the same and follows its own laws. And those laws are none of our business. Think of the birds flying south for the winter, cranes for instance. They fly on and on and on, and it doesn't matter what ideas, big or small, they may have buzzing inside their heads, they'll still keep on flying without ever knowing why they do it or where they're going. They fly on and on, and what if they do throw up a few philosophers? Let them keep their philosophy so long as they don't stop flying.

MASHA But what's the point of it all?

TUZENBAKH The point? Look, it's snowing out there. What's the point of that?[1]

Absolute absurdity is incapable of tragic resolution. It is a predicament so irredeemable that it can only be *arraigned* (whether glumly or with lacerating mirth), or kicked against with existentialist histrionics:

THE TUTOR ...This Argos is a nightmare city. Squeals of terror everywhere, people who panic the moment they set eyes on you, and scurry to cover. Like black beetles, down the glaring streets. Pfoo! I can't think how you bear it—this emptiness, the shimmering air, that fierce sun overhead. What's deadlier than the sun?

ORESTES I was born here.[2]

Sartre's Orestes—unlike Aeschylus's—has to *invent* human values from scratch. His predicament, therefore, can have no inherent meaning—not even that of a tragic victim or questioner; his heroism belongs to melodrama; the 'emptiness' and 'deadly' sun of his Argos will remain what they were when he finally 'strides into the light' with his big, self-dramatizing words while 'the Furies fling themselves after him'.

---

[1] *Three Sisters*, Act II.
[2] Jean-Paul Sartre, *The Flies* (translated by Stuart Gilbert), Act I.

Chekhov's inability to rest either in tragic meanings or in a post-tragic writing off of ultimate meanings led him, as we saw, into various experiments in pseudo-comedy. But absurdity is no remedy for the Absurd, and his achieved effects are almost indistinguishable from 'arraignments'.

Amazingly, Chekhov not only included *Three Sisters* among the plays he thought of as comedies but repeatedly insisted on its being a 'gay comedy' or even a 'farce'.[1] Thus it is all the more fascinating to ponder two revisions of the last scene, both in response to other people's difficulties in rehearsal. The first is a cut in Masha's last speech, now reading: 'Oh, listen to the band. They're all leaving us, and one has gone right away and will never, never come back, and we shall be left alone to begin our lives again. We must go on living, we must'. After 'left alone to begin our lives again' the original draft continued:

I shall go on living, my dears. One must live. [*Looks upwards.*] There are migrating birds up there, they fly past every spring and autumn, they've been doing it for thousands of years and they don't know why. But they fly on and they'll go on flying for ages and ages, for many thousand years, until in the end God reveals his mystery to them.[2]

The second change is a cut in the final stage direction, three or four lines from the end (following '*The music becomes fainter and fainter*'):

There is a noise at the back of the stage. A crowd can be seen as the body of the baron, who has been killed in the duel, is carried past.[3]

[1] See *The Oxford Chekhov*, vol. III, Appendix, pp. 314 and 316.
[2] *Ibid.*, p. 311.　　　　　　[3] *Ibid.*

With the first of these passages one hardly knows whether to attach more importance to the ways in which it picks up the Tuzenbakh–Masha exchange of Act II quoted above[1] (does Masha really believe what she says here—and, even if she does, is she nearer the mark than Tuzenbakh?) or to Chekhov's casual dropping of the passage simply because Olga Knipper, who played the part, found it 'difficult to say'.

The second cut—in view of Stanislavsky's practical problem: 'the sisters have got to see the corpse. What are they to do?'—corresponds to Chekhov's own misgivings on this point. And since the baron's death has already been reported shortly before, the point may in a sense not be so important. Yet the fact that Chekhov was at one time willing to admit the physical presentation of the corpse, amidst all the other grave notes of this scene, further heightens the strangeness of his 'gay comedy' notion.

Thus, when we consider Chekhov's repeated indignant protest 'But what I wrote was a farce',[2] it is difficult not to feel that his marvellous creative compassion was so in tension with an *a priori* determination to deliver a hopeful verdict on life as to exact an 'optimism' indistinguishable from callousness. Perhaps this impossible marriage of tender realistic sympathy with a toughly wilful—almost Olympian, almost cynical—detachment is the essential matrix of Chekhov's art—and of his special contemporary significance. It only needs the collapse—the inevitable delayed breakdown—of this cynically defended commit-

[1] pp. 152–3, above. [2] *The Oxford Chekhov*, vol. III, p. 316.

ment to hope to transmute his idiom into the sheer
to desperate farce of our own time.

From Shakespeare's Pascalian *catharsis* within despair to
Beckett's turning and turning within the debris of absolute
hope the line runs, critically, through Chekhov. Whatever
Chekhov may have been intent on, he was not, in his
maturity, a plausible gay comedian, but the genius of
hesitancy between tragic *catharsis* and post-tragic farce.
When he himself sought to recreate an uncompromisingly
'tragic' harmony he produced the conclusion of *Uncle
Vanya*. But at any rate Chekhov's efforts to resolve, by
hook or by crook, the tragic situations confronting him
were an uncompromising attempt to take life as it is—and
with an ultimate serious hopefulness. We have moved on
since. The Chekhovian heritage of pseudo-comedy is now
being turned inside out in those proverbial—almost pop-
art—dustbins of the Absurd, while an ever lengthening
line of practical jokers, from Jean Anouilh to Ionesco and
Pinter and Arrabal, are killing themselves with laughter
over the posthumous reflexes of tragic exaltation. Even
T. S. Eliot found it necessary, in his last phase, to deliver
his clerkly admonitions from the solid foundation of *The
Importance of Being Earnest*. But then, anyway, what can
one do but laugh in an era in which the *Daily Telegraph*
was able to report:

The three-day atomic defence test in the US estimates
'casualties' at 14,750,000, including 6,200,000 dead. The number of 'homeless' is put at 25 million. On the credit side is
the saving of 5,250,000...by evacuation from 24 of the 61
cities under attack. The general conclusion was that this would
not mean a general collapse; the war could still go on.

The Extreme Verge

After all, in the meantime, like Estragon and Vladimir—
or for that matter their Chekhovian forebears—we have
go on living.

And yet, there is another kind of response, another kind
of language, that might yet be re-learned—a language no
less laughter-torn than ours, but that, by its loyal insistence
upon what laughter would disown, can release the heart's
most radical reasons—a language that, at its greatest, can
cry:

> If that the heavens do not their visible spirits
> Send quickly down to tame these vile offences,
> It will come,
> Humanity must perforce prey on itself,
> Like monsters of the deep.

We shall either re-learn this kind of language, or perish.

5

'THE COCKTAIL PARTY'

Eliot's *Cocktail Party* has a significance far greater than its achievements as a work of art might seem to warrant. Failures, among the works of a great writer, have to be taken seriously; especially if he is such a highly deliberate and self-critical one as T. S. Eliot. It is not merely that, whatever their limitations, such works are nevertheless likely to be of considerable intrinsic interest, but that they will almost inevitably throw light on other aspects of his artistic career. Further, the play's material scope is obviously of the widest serious concern. It is, after all, facing ranges of 'problems' that matter—and doing so with uncompromising decisiveness. This decisiveness may reveal unacceptable foundations; still, even rejection pre-supposes tangible formulation at some stage, and one is glad to have such an authoritative one. For better or worse *The Cocktail Party* occupies a pivotal place among Eliot's poetic dramas. And since, moreover, its author is also the author of *The Waste Land* and *Four Quartets*, we may also expect it to be indirectly illuminating and perhaps, in some respects, to modify our view of his poetry as a whole.

I

A brief interpretative summary will be necessary as a basis for discussion. It is suggested that something on the follow-ing lines emerges from the pattern of the play:

1. Human relations are either permeated by illusion or, disillusioned, lacking in 'ecstasy'. (i) They are illusory: either because they are rooted in idealizations of the other (as Celia idealizes Edward), or sheer incomprehension of the other (as Peter's spurious understanding of Celia); or self-deception (as Edward's relation to Celia, and—previously—to Lavinia; there is also an element of self-deception in Peter's incomprehension of Celia, on whom he projects his own self-idealization). (ii) If not illusory, they are lacking in 'ecstasy', since they must then grow out of active disillusionment—a state at which all the above characters arrive, and which appears also to be the foundation of Sir Henry Harcourt-Reilly's centrally privileged personality.

2. This state of affairs is not contingent on individual experience; it is part of 'the human condition' (Reilly's phrase) which, at the level of human relations, is one of inescapable aloneness.

REILLY   So you want to see no one?
CELIA   No...it isn't that I *want* to be alone,
    But that everyone's alone—or so it seems to me.
    They make noises, and think they are talking to each
       other;
    They make faces, and think they understand each other.
    And I'm sure that they don't. Is that a delusion?
REILLY   A delusion is something we must return from.
    There are other states of mind which we take to be
       delusion,
    But which we have to accept and go on from.

3. 'Going on' from this 'state of mind' accordingly

resolves itself into an *acceptance* of this aloneness—into making 'the best of a bad job':

EDWARD   Lavinia, we must make the best of a bad job.
          That is what he means.
REILLY   When you find, Mr. Chamberlayne,
          The best of a bad job is all any of us make of it—
          Except of course, the saints—such as those who go
          To the sanatorium—you will forget this phrase,
          And in forgetting it will alter the condition.

—Though 'the condition' for all such is to:

                          remember
          The vision they have had, but they cease to regret it,
          Maintain themselves by the common routine,
          Learn to avoid excessive expectation,
          Become tolerant of themselves and others,
          Giving and taking, in the usual actions
          What there is to give and take. They do not repine...

which, of course, is the 'condition'—the world of panto-mime and cocktail parties—in which the Chamberlaynes are left at the end of the play; and, in his different way, Peter, maintaining himself by the common routine at Boltwell ('with a team of experts'), doing a good job of work on a second-rate film:

PETER   I suppose I didn't know her,
          I didn't understand her. I understand nothing.
REILLY   You understand your *métier*, Mr. Quilpe—
          Which is the most that any of us can ask for.

Except of course, the saints—such as those who go to the sanatorium!

    4. And this, heroic sanctity, is offered as the *only* alter-

native to making 'the best of a bad job' at the level of personal relations or of maintaining oneself 'by the common routine'—at Boltwell or elsewhere. That is why it is here rooted in

> The kind of faith that issues from despair.

'Communion' is possible only with God. Those who take the 'other' way can '*forget* their loneliness' (they cannot escape it);

> You will not forget yours.
> Each way means loneliness—and communion.
> Both ways avoid the final desolation
> Of solitude in the phantasmal world
> Of imagination, shuffling memories and desires.

The dichotomy is thus explicitly made absolute. The two ways—

> Neither way is better.
> Both are necessary. It is also necessary
> To make a choice between them—

each involving 'loneliness', are sharply opposed to any attempted 'communion' at other levels. Desire for such communion is vain. Everyone's alone—except for the transcendent; human relations have no intrinsic reality or value: their only value (like that of heroic sanctity) is *instrumental*, leading (provided we can accept them as valueless in themselves!)

> towards possession
> Of what you have sought for in the wrong place.

And 'the wrong place' covers a wide area, to be sure: the entire field of values in time, in so far as they are pursued in and for themselves. It is the futility of such a pursuit which the earlier part of the play seeks to establish.

These attempts—the usual stuff of life—are revealed as leading to the familiar entanglements of conventional comedy, or to the brink of tragedy and despair: indeed, but for Reilly and his assistants, to

> the final desolation
> Of solitude in the phantasmal world
> Of imagination, shuffling memories and desires.

For it is in this 'phantasmal world' that they inhere. Real communion can only be won by a free acceptance of 'loneliness' one 'way' or another—complete surrender of temporal fruition.

5. The final implication is surely that Time is entirely corrupt: not merely fallen and imperfect, and finally subject to the Eternal, but destitute of any intrinsic positive significance. Those who

> do not repine;
> Are contented with the morning that separates
> And with the evening that brings together
> For casual talk before the fire
> Two people who know they do not understand each other,
> Breeding children whom they do not understand
> And who will never understand them—

lead 'a good life', Reilly assures Celia;

> Though you will not know how good
> Till you come to the end.

Its goodness, that is, is exclusively a moral one—and 'moral' in the narrowest of ways:

> In a world of lunacy,
> Violence, stupidity, greed...it is a good life.

'Good', here, surely for what it will bring—when 'you
come to the end'; hardly for what it *is*: to seek its goodness partly in what it is would be to seek 'in the wrong
place'. Love, full-blooded, full-spirited love of another
creature, has emerged as either a projection of the self,
or a projection of infinite religious aspirations, into finite
symbols for ever removed from all genuine relation. The
sort of natural happiness people look for in human relationships is thus not merely presented as illusory: but as
a narcissist indulgence in a 'phantasmal world' of self-
reflection, or a pseudo-religious inflation of equally 'phantasmal' temporal existents. And it is not merely specifically
misguided pursuits of such happiness that are in question
but the pursuit as such, wherever it is of an immediate
fulfilment. And so when Celia asks:

> Can we only love
> Something created by our own imagination?
> Are we all in fact unloving and unlovable?
> Then one *is* alone, and if one is alone
> Then lover and beloved are equally unreal
> And the dreamer is no more real than his dreams—

Reilly, though he does not directly assent, does not challenge the suggestion. And the two exclusive alternatives
he offers to the unperceived solitude of illusion are the
loneliness of a disillusioned domesticity, so innocent of
'phantasy' that
> you will not know how good
> Till you come to the end—

and the loneliness of a 'faith that issues from despair',
whose
> way leads towards possession
> Of what you have sought for in the wrong place.

The possibility of expunging 'illusion' and yet retaining 'ecstasy', of raising *having* to *being*, *I-It* to *I-Thou*, within the limits of the created universe, is not allowed to intrude. *Here is a place of disaffection.*

II

The disturbing conclusion emerges that *The Cocktail Party* is (unwittingly) a Manichean play. Its vision is not that of a humane—'Incarnational' and 'sacramental'—Christianity, but approximates to a radical division of existence into spheres of Nature and Transcendence sharply separated from each other: where the transcendent is not merely approached by way of the disclosure of Nature's essential imperfections, but finally embraced as a—literally —*desperate alternative* to the latter's graceless essence.

Whatever the 'intention' (and at any rate we may be sure that this does not include the crystallization of Manichean attitudes) some such result seems indubitably present to us in the play. It is as if, caught in the boiling-bitter flood of life-revulsion that has gathered to such enormity in our time, Eliot, swept along on its crest, were at the same time composedly—and even somewhat primly— delivering an authoritative sermon on Hope. There is all but no attempt to qualify the sense of self-imprisonment, the desolate unreality of disenchanted existence *here and now*: where one has

> no delusions—
> Except that the world I live in seems all a delusion;

—where

> Nothing again can either hurt or heal

164

—and all is

> Dry, endless, meaningless, inhuman—

like a heap of broken 'phantasmal' Thou's. 'The horror and the boredom' (significant key words in Eliot's criticism) are not merely accepted, as products of the disasters and inadequacies of a plane of being which is nevertheless gifted with life and reality, but are apparently accepted *as sovereign and exclusive principles of temporal existence*. So that those at last 'stripped naked to their souls', if not eligible for 'the sanatorium', will at best

> Maintain themselves by the common routine,

in a world of committees, film-making, drawing-room relationships and immaculate husbandly compliments about dresses—

> *Before* a party! And that's when one needs them.

Even if 'the vision they have had' is no longer regretted, 'the horror and the boredom' would appear to be endemic.

In his essay on Matthew Arnold, Eliot intimately associates 'the horror and the boredom' with a third term:

It is an advantage to mankind in general to live in a beautiful world; that no one can doubt. But for the poet is it so important? We mean all sorts of things, I know, by Beauty. But the essential advantage for a poet is not to have a beautiful world with which to deal: it is to be able to see beneath both beauty and ugliness; to see the boredom, and the horror, and the glory.

To see beneath both beauty and ugliness; to see the boredom, and the horror, and the glory is a fitting description of Eliot's own finest poetic achievements. But if 'to have a beautiful world with which to deal' is indeed no 'essential advantage for a poet', nevertheless, there are times and conditions 'that seem unpropitious', and Eliot's own achievements are hard won indeed, and only barely less hard to preserve. Thus it seems essential that Eliot's three features should be joined in organic interaction: it is this which gives them their combined authority and distinction as a characterization of experience at these abysmal levels. For 'the horror' would not be so horrifying, 'the boredom' not so desperately empty, but for 'the glory' from which they have sprung and which still sustains and contains them; nor 'the glory' so potently triumphant and ecstatic but for 'the horror and the boredom' that have risen from its soil, as its perpetual challenge. 'The vision of the horror and the glory was denied to Arnold', Eliot says, 'but he knew something of the boredom'. Eliot certainly knew all three; but in *The Cocktail Party* there is no vision of glory, although it reiterates something of the boredom and the horror.

Or rather, such 'glory' as there is evoked in this play— entering through

The kind of faith that issues from despair—

is for ever disjoined from the immediate apprehensions of the *here-and-now* (we need to be *told*, apparently, even that Celia's martyrdom 'was triumphant'), for ever reserved in a *beyond*—which holds out Hope, for the beyond; which invests with instrumental ('moral') value states of being devoid of all that could make them valuable in themselves; but which appears unwilling, or unable, to

reclaim for transformation the horror and the boredom
of this prodigious cocktail party—

> Life is very long

—evidencing no tendency to 'redeem the time'.

III

This drift towards Manicheism—in its essential revulsion
from life, 'yoked by violence' to a transcendental affirmation of Hope—is as apparent in the play's distinctive
technical qualities as in the more direct analytic formulations of its vision that have so far been stressed.

Indeed, to speak of 'analytic formulations' seems a
peculiarly fitting procedure in a discussion of this play.
For one of its most pervasive, and obtrusive, features is
its leaning towards the undramatic on the one hand, and
towards the prosaic on the other. Dramatic and poetic
immediacy, the vital complexity of an *embodied* vision—
rooted in some integral affirmation, and accordingly
charged with creative responsiveness to immediate existence—is here either at a discount, or simply beyond
possibility of attainment. And so, too, it is not for nothing
that this above all tragically weighted play should seek
expression in an ostensibly 'comic' framework. For the
fullness of tragedy can impinge only in the fullness of a
world of 'glory'—a world whose here-and-now are infinitely meaningful and precious. As its consummation in
the Cross, the tragedy of the Word *made Flesh*, tragedy
can exist, can bring tragic purgation, only in and to a
world that is *purgeable*—a world that, when all has been

faced, yet remains planted in inexhaustible depths of beauty and worth.

Celia is less than tragic, and so less than triumphant. Tragically triumphant she ought to be, and Reilly does not omit to announce how we are meant to take her. But like the other characters of the play, Celia—the experience that is Celia—is not sufficiently acted out to sustain an evolving tragic immediacy. Some of her most central efforts of self-definition fail to condense into a worthy poetic presence:

> For what happened is remembered like a dream
> In which one is exalted by intensity of loving
> In the spirit, a vibration of delight
> Without desire, for desire is fulfilled
> In the delight of loving. A state one does not know
> When awake...

—the *Four Quartets*, as it were, turned into jargon and unsubstantiated gestures. The absoluteness of her despair is neither rooted in a relationship proportionately substantiated to begin with, nor allowed to achieve its own transforming insights and tragic witness. Thus there is no sufficient 'objective correlative' behind the play to give it sustained tragic authority (and this lack is felt with much greater urgency than it is in *Hamlet*—in the course of whose condemnation, it will be remembered, Eliot coined this useful critical term). Instead, Reilly not only short-circuits the tragic process, but freezes Celia's momentary impulse to universalize her disillusionment into a definitive, authorized universality. It is not, presumably, suggested that *Hamlet* falls short to such an extent as this. But perhaps there may be some causal similarity in the shortcomings of the two works. In *Hamlet*, Eliot suggests, Shakespeare 'attempted to express the inexpressibly horrible'; while the tragic materials that lay to his hand were, moreover, peculiarly intolerant to the expression of this recoiling vision. Nihilism, we may generally say, tends to frustrate even its own orderly articulation, and least of all can it find expression in tragic terms. Nihilism is not tragic. It is the antithesis of tragedy—of tragic horror as of tragic glory; it has supped full of horrors (is not Macbeth's tragedy precisely his annihilation within himself of all that makes tragedy possible?): only boredom, and the horror of boredom—

> what you brought with you:
> The shadow of desires of desires—

remains. And *The Cocktail Party* presents us with a kind of nihilism; since a nihilistic vision of life remains none the less nihilistic for being pinned to a universe of trans-cendental affirmation incarcerated in eternity—for ever *beyond* tomorrow's cocktail parties, and tomorrow's drives to Boltwell, and tomorrow's unecstatic nights at home.

And so *The Cocktail Party* is offered not as a tragedy but as 'a comedy' superimposed upon tragic hints and guesses. Such a structure might conceivably serve as a potent means of deepening, and extending, a fundamen-tally tragic vision. Here, however, one is aware of it mainly as the defensive refinement of a dramatic utterance rarely adequate in dramatization, which thus cannot attain to tragic stature. Nor can this structure actually save the play from the bathos of 'intentions' merely intended. Failing in organic contact, the two levels are even in principle precluded from genuinely qualifying each other; whilst in fact at the same time each also fails within its own terms. It is not merely Celia and the evocations surrounding her tragedy that are insufficiently realized. Edward, Lavinia and Peter (whether regarded in a 'comic' or a 'tragic' perspective) do not let us forget that they are illustrations. And it must be confessed that Julia and Alex, with their astonishing feats of transformation from the most obedient of West-End stock types to those symbols-of-something-or-other somehow-or-other actual and active within a world of stock types, and Sir Henry Harcourt-Reilly himself—the Stranger, the One-eyed, a sort of ecumenical Harley Street Tiresias, with an unexpected devotion to Shelley—disturb, and sometimes appeal to us, in ways that cannot have been contemplated by the author.

The position of the 'Guardians' is, of course, crucial in the organization of the play. Clearly we are intended to accept them in terms of the poetic-dramatic conventions supplied by the play itself; and indeed the gradual unfolding of common-place incidents and personages into typical and symbolic significances is as much an aspect of the play's *theatrical* impact as of the ultimate burden of its 'meaning'. Its suspense and surprise values and structural ironies lean heavily upon this symbol-charged mysteriousness of its protagonists and framework, upon our diligent accumulation of clues ('Who is this "Stranger", how does he know all this?'; 'but why "*Gin and water*"?';

'So *that's* what "the Sanatorium" is !'; 'then Reilly must be... !') and we undoubtedly derive a certain satisfaction from this sort of pursuit, especially if we have backed pretty well the right ideas most of the time. Nevertheless, we seem to be left with a number of difficulties—both with regard to the straightforward issue of what is 'actually' going on (or 'who' it is we have in front of us) and what is 'symbolically' represented by it all. For 'fact' and 'symbol' in this play seem to be kept almost aggressively distinct, and yet at the same time not only to merge, but to disappear into each other without warning. Thus the atmosphere of mystery informing the play often thickens into something more akin to mystification. We know, of course, in a broad sort of a way, what the 'Guardians' *stand for*. But surely we are entitled to ask what Reilly, and Alex and Julia, 'really' *are*: it is, after all, as 'real' characters, who take gin, or whisky, or champagne in an elegant West End flat, that they are introduced to us. Are they, for instance, subsequent to first impressions, in any sense individuals at all—or just a collective evocation of the Church? If individuals, have they deliberately planned the whole affair from the outset, specializing in this kind of campaign (as their private exchanges and their proposed descent upon 'the Gunnings' following the Chamberlayne episode would seem to suggest)? But in that case, what is the capacity in which all this is done; and how is it that Alex and Julia are to all the world the genial amateur cook (also

the sort of person
Who would know the right doctors, as well as the right shops)

and the shamelessly inquisitive *enfant terrible* of Act I? Is it because that is how they—or whatever is represented by them—appear to a foolish world that judges, alas, by appearances; or because they deliberately enact these parts in accordance with some secret missionary strategy? If the former, are appearances and first impressions not a little *too* deceptive here?; if the latter, why this unrivalled Machiavellian tortuousness in going about their tasks?— Or, if perhaps it is felt that we are not called upon to ask questions of this kind relative to poetic drama, well, just what *is* the precise significance, literal and symbolic, of the 'Guardians' in the play, why are the two planes kept so sharply divorced? And then how is the symbolic reality represented by the 'Guardians' to be envisaged as impinging upon the obstinately literal facts of a world of Chamberlaynes and Gunnings? Nothing seems established but the dissociated evocation of two planes: what precisely is represented by each, and, *a fortiori*, how they are conceived as interacting, does not emerge with any clarity from the text.

May this defectiveness not be a technical symptom of the dissociated attitude towards temporal and spiritual that we have already discussed? Mr John Peter has pointed out the relationship between the internal tension within the characters of Alex and Julia and the more general tension pervading the play:

To make the contrast between the Julia of the real world and the Julia of the spiritual world so gross is only to increase that tension to a point at which the play begins to tear apart. Where the play should be forcing us to see the interdependence

of the two worlds, forcing us to admit that the spiritual underlies and informs the actual, we get instead the impression that
they are so distinct, so little related, that to move from one
to the other is like putting on an impenetrable disguise...
That the deliberate convention of 'inner selves' should at first
sight give an impression of simple ineptitude is thus not its
chief defect. What is serious is that in another way it is itself
inept, and draws attention to a material dichotomy which it
was part of the business of the dramatist to dissolve or remove.[1]

Surely it is right and important to relate the 'dichotomy'
within the 'Guardians' to the 'tension' informing the
play as a whole. It may, however, be suggested that
what occasions this tearing apart is not merely the 'material
dichotomy' rooted, as Mr Peter holds, in the difficulty
of effecting 'the necessary emotional synthesis between
the world of ideas, of belief, in which the topics discussed
may be said to exist, and the mundane world of taxis and
boiled eggs which is the *milieu* of the characters'. For
although such a difficulty is admittedly inherent in the
task of relating 'belief' to such a *milieu*, it did not prove
too much for the poet elsewhere in his works; and here
there was at any rate no need to 'draw attention' to the
difficulty by means of the convention we are considering.
On the face of it, certainly as far as Alex and Julia are
concerned, the convention seems purely gratuitous. There
would therefore seem to be some force in the suggestion
that the dichotomy to which the play 'draws attention'
in this way is not primarily that between the contemporary material *milieu* and the world of ideas and 'belief',
but between the World and the Flesh as such and spiritual

[1] *Scrutiny*, vol. XVII (Spring 1950), p. 65.

existence, between Nature and Grace; and that *this* dichotomy is here not 'dissolved or removed' because, so far from demanding a fusion of temporal and spiritual experience, the pressures seeking utterance in this play tend precisely towards their divorce.

To the play's avoidance of full 'tragedy' (since tragedy requires a full-blooded, positive concern for the here-and-now) and the oddly bifurcated presentation of Alex and Julia, we may finally relate, as symptoms of its negative vision of life, the general 'abstractness' of the play's dramatic framework as well as of its poetic texture.

The vision of *The Cocktail Party* lacks body. It is neither actualized as a whole, in terms of 'dramatic' categories, nor pulsating locally with sufficient poetic intensity.[1] We have already, in passing, touched upon one or two aspects of these deficiencies. It remains to stress the peculiar tech-

[1] This poetic inadequacy seems to be quite distinct from Eliot's concern (as described in his Spencer Memorial Lecture, on *Poetry and Drama*) to evolve 'a form of versification and an idiom which would serve all my purposes without recourse to prose, and be capable of unbroken transition between the most intense speech and the most relaxed dialogue' and 'to avoid poetry which would not stand the test of strict dramatic utility'. For often when the play does approach 'intensity'—as in some of Reilly's speeches and Celia's—the verse tends to be overlaid with a series of stiffly external, rootless images, not energized from any vital centre, or to abandon any attempt at imaginative definition, giving way to rhetorical inflation. (Cf. p. 168 above.) One cannot but deplore the loss, from *The Cocktail Party* onwards, of the confident poetic vigour at work, in different forms, in *Murder in the Cathedral* and *The Family Reunion*. Not only Eliot's own career as a dramatist, but modern English drama as a whole, might have developed very differently if he could have related himself more positively to the *Family Reunion*—which, with all its flaws, seems to me a major original achievement—and a possible point of departure for future writers.

nical use made of the character of Reilly, who seems to be not so much a dramatic figure as an alternative to drama. As the action unfolds, Reilly reveals himself as not merely presiding over the play, stage-managing it (rather like the Duke, in *Measure for Measure*) but more and more reveals himself as *being* the play—having perceived much and foretold the rest; and whoever he may happen to be fixing in his gaze (a gaze not open to deception) he in fact is invariably addressing *us*—talking to us through, or over the shoulders of, his clients:

EDWARD   And since then, I have realised
    That mine is a very unusual case.
REILLY   All cases are unique, and very similar to others.

You! — hypocrite lecteur! — mon semblable, — mon frère!
(Though, perhaps, we cannot really be so sure of 'mon frère' here.) Whether Sir Henry is analysing Edward and Lavinia, or confirming Celia's analyses of life with his authority, or telling Peter that he understands his *métier*—

    Which is the most that any of us can ask for

—it is clear that the subjects of his admonitions remain all the time in the obscurity of the auditorium: there is not enough substance in the personages who occasion his observations to deflect these to a genuinely dramatic angle, nor does he himself ever spring to spontaneous dramatic life. The device of Reilly's consulting-room, and the convergence of the 'plot' towards the definitions propounded there, is a final abdication from drama.

IV

The difficulties of re-vitalizing poetic drama under contemporary conditions have often been discussed—notably by Eliot himself; and they may be specially acute for poets with urgent religious or philosophical commitments. If, however, our examination of *The Cocktail Party* is valid, the play's deficiencies reflect not merely these difficulties but, more essentially, an underlying failure of outlook.

A diagnosis of this failure could serve as a favourable point of observation from which Eliot's work as a whole might be reviewed. Throughout his development as a poet, Eliot was peculiarly consistent in his preoccupations, and whatever the changes that characterize his work—in emphasis, or commitment, or breadth of vision—its unity is assured, and must affect not only our view of his output as a whole but our understanding and evaluation of each constituent part. *Prufrock* and *The Waste Land* appear in a new perspective, and perhaps acquire a new dimension, in the context of *Ash Wednesday* and *Four Quartets* (which, in turn, could not be fully appreciated without reference to these preceding works). And *The Cocktail Party* (more so, I think, than any of his other plays) may help us to fuller insights into the central consciousness behind the works, and perhaps direct us towards some adjustments in our total response.

To attempt anything like a full review of Eliot's work falls outside the scope of this essay, but the lines on which such a review might proceed will perhaps already be apparent. *The Cocktail Party*, so essentially post-*Quartets*

in intellectual viewpoint and intention, is much more akin
in involuntary accent to:

> For I have known them all already, known them all—
> Have known the evenings, mornings, afternoons...

or to:

> The woman keeps the kitchen, makes tea,
> Sneezes at evening, poking the peevish gutter.
>   I an old man,
> A dull head among windy spaces...

than it is to:

>   the spring time
>   But not in time's covenant

—by which 'the horror and the boredom' culminating
in *The Hollow Men* might have seemed to be finally
transcended. And so the attitudes apparently won through
to in *Ash Wednesday* and *Four Quartets* seem, in retrospect,
more precarious than used to be assumed and invite a renewed examination in this light; though the extent of
their achievement stands out all the more impressively
under conditions so 'unpropitious'.

While it seems evident, now, that a religious effort—

>   having to construct something
> Upon which to rejoice—

informs even the earliest of Eliot's published verse, the
'stony rubbish' of the *Waste Land* survives, side by side
with the rose garden of *Burnt Norton*, throughout much
of the later work:

Eructation of unhealthy souls
Into the faded air, the torpid

'The Cocktail Party'

Driven on the wind that sweeps the gloomy hills of London,
Hampstead and Clerkenwell, Campden and Putney,
Highgate, Primrose and Ludgate...

The *Ariel Poems* had introduced 'a Birth, certainly', but—
with the exception of *Marina*—had brought no renewal
of vital energy; on the contrary, emotionally they consummate the dryness of the preceding phase. In *Ash
Wednesday* the entire scale is sounded, from the renuncia-
tion, at one level, of 'The infirm glory of the positive
hour'—

There, where trees flower, and springs flow, for there is
  nothing again

—through the torment

> Under the vapour in the fetid air
> Struggling with the devil of the stairs who wears
> The deceitful face of hope and of despair

—to 'the third stair', and the beginnings of *restoration* of
'the years' ('where trees flower, and springs flow') themselves:

Here are the years that walk between, bearing
Away the fiddles and the flutes, restoring
One who moves in the time between sleep and waking,
  wearing

White light folded, sheathed about her, folded.
The new years walk, restoring,
Through a bright cloud of tears, the years, restoring
With a new verse the ancient rhyme. Redeem
The time. Redeem
The unread vision in the higher dream
While jewelled unicorns draw by the gilded hearse.

This wonderfully potent and delicate poise—between time as 'bearing / *Away* the fiddles and the flutes' and time (the line divisions are richly suggestive throughout) as simply '*bearing*' them; between its 'cloud of tears' and their restoring *brightness*; between the 'hearse' and the hearse's splendour and redeeming ('unicorn'-drawn) movement —evidently proved no less difficult to hold than to achieve. For although its tensions and counterpoises are embodied with complete mastery in the *Quartets*, there the struggle towards wholeness—

> not less of love but expanding
> Of love beyond desire, and so liberation
> From the future as well as the past—

seems to find its most complete fulfilment at the less directly 'personal' levels of experience, those of social and historical involvement, which form such an important element in them; there is relatively less stress upon such specifically 'personal' struggles as precede, and follow, the *Quartets* (and as must surely be the testing-points of the kind of dynamic equilibrium arrived at). And in so far as these more intimate experiences are accorded emphasis here, they tend to be so essentially absorbed into the de-personalizing medium of the poetry that it is uncertain whether this does not involve some degree of *evasion* of personal problems, as well as a movement towards their solution. At any rate, the

> echoed ecstasy
> Not lost but requiring
>
> —Whispers of running streams, and winter lightning,
> The wild thyme unseen, and the wild strawberry,

> The laughter in the garden, echoed ecstasy
> Not lost but requiring, pointing to the agony
> Of death and birth—

reverts, in the directly 'personal' atmosphere of *The Cocktail Party*, to a *romantic* 'ecstasy',

> remembered like a dream
> In which one is exalted in intensity of loving
> In the spirit, a vibration of delight
> Without desire, for desire is fulfilled
> In the delight of loving—

leaving—inevitably and catastrophically '*lost*'—only

> the inconsolable memory
> Of the treasure I went into the forest to find.

We are thus thrust back, from the richly orchestrated 'hints and guesses' and the complex movement towards their assimilation in the *Quartets*, to the lilac and the re-awakening dull roots where April is the cruellest month. 'Memory and desire', the living monuments of romantic ecstasy and romantic frustration, remain potent constituents in the poet's developing vision. It is essentially the apprehension, and collapse, of a romantic beatitude, confrontation with

> The final desolation
> Of solitude in the phantasmal world
> Of imagination, shuffling memories and desires

that impels the religious energies in this play.

Perhaps there is more of the unwilling, inverted romantic in Eliot than has been recognized. Indeed, the development of his art might be interpreted as a unified, and heroic, struggle with an inherited romanticism—which he disowned from the outset, but never completely succeeded in mastering. Even the superb and immensely influential manifesto 'Tradition and the Individual Talent', protesting the essential 'impersonality' of poetry ('But, of course, only those who have personality and emotions know what it is to want to escape from these things') should perhaps be read in this light. From *Prufrock* to the *Hollow Men* we would thus have not a purely 'impersonal' statement of the modern plight but, underpinning it, a symbolist exposition of the romantic 'problem'. *Ash Wednesday* may then be Eliot's nearest approach towards its 'solution' in religious terms. The *Four Quartets*, in spite of their astonishing range and depth of vision, achieve their balance at the cost of a certain reticence at the most 'personal' levels:

> There is a time for the evening under starlight
> A time for the evening under lamplight
> (The evening with the photograph album)

—but not much time:

> Love is most nearly itself
> When here and now cease to matter

—and indeed, although (or because) 'history is a pattern of timeless moments',

> Here or there does not matter.

In *The Cocktail Party* the specifically 'personal' element is re-emphasized, but instead of even attempting an integral solution it proceeds to a radical bifucation of reality; merely offering 'ways'—devoid of any intrinsic value—which will lead

towards possession
Of what you sought for in *the wrong place*.

The 'garden in the desert' is now hermetically walled in.

It is in the light of this dissociation that the varying degrees of achievement in Eliot's poetic career are best evaluated. *The Confidential Clerk* and *The Elder Statesman* seem deliberately, and admirably, engaged in seeking to break down this wall (indeed, the former even has an actual 'garden' figuring prominently in the play's imagery, as well as in one of the characters' domestic background). But ultimately this is as much a matter of poetic realization as of spiritual endeavour. And, since the abandonment of the frankly 'poetic' resources of *Murder in the Cathedral* and *The Family Reunion*, in *The Cocktail Party*, the 'garden' seems hardly sufficiently potent to re-fertilize, and transform, the barren city.

6

HUMANISM AND TRAGIC
REDEMPTION

When George Steiner announced *The Death of Tragedy*, in 1961, it was already somewhat unclear whether tragedy was said to be dead or dying, or in fact on the way to being reborn. Since then, Leo Aylen's *Greek Tragedy and the Modern World*[1] has challengingly affirmed the possibility of actual equivalents to Greek tragedy in our time. Lastly, Raymond Williams flatly entitles his own critical diagnosis: *Modern Tragedy*.[2]

These questions of course extend far beyond the theatre. Ultimately they concern the entire substance of our culture, and especially our age's increasing estrangement from religion. For tragedy—whether Greek, mediaeval, Elizabethan or neo-classical—has, typically, sprung from societies rooted in religion; although the greatest moments of tragic art were precisely those moments when received beliefs stood under radical historical challenge. To ask why traditional tragic forms have increasingly been abandoned in the theatre of our time is, thus, to raise questions we might otherwise not even be able to formulate about our epoch's relations to religion—and about the resources of humanist faith.

Raymond Williams's confrontation of these questions seems to me crucial, in several ways. Unmistakably at the

[1] London, 1964.   [2] London, 1966.

growing-point of humanist consciousness, his work is at once a critique of tragic theory, a socio-critical map of modern tragic literature, and a re-assertion in depth of revolutionary imperatives in the face of objections to revolution truly wrestled with. Significantly, the book concludes not with any theoretical summing up but with an actual drama of revolution. However this play should be assessed as an imaginative creation in its own right (it was conceived before the discursive material), it certainly helps to define, and to bring to the test, the dialectical thrust of the book as a whole. There is every reason to think that *Modern Tragedy* will remain a living source of understanding and human choice, however we may, in time, live through these questions.

Williams starts from the recognition that, on the one hand, 'tragedy' stands for an imposing, complex tradition of art and theory, exacting tribute from any disciplined use of the term, and that, on the other hand, there is something strange and disorientating about the conventional academic gloss that would deny to 'mere suffering' —'everyday tragedies' in private or social life—any claim to being 'genuinely tragic'. Matters of actual life and death are thus dissociated from tragic concepts; life is, critically, stripped of the significances art professes to discover in it; and an age as deeply involved in tragic experience, and as rich and engrossed in tragic writing, as our own, is seriously in doubt whether tragedy has not died.

Williams's refusal to accept this semantic schizophrenia as a necessary sacrifice to literary tradition is surely irreversible:

Humanism and Tragic Redemption

What is more deeply in question is a particular kind and particular interpretation of death and suffering. Certain events and responses are tragic, and others not. By sheer authority, and from our natural eagerness to learn, it is possible for this to be said and repeated, without real challenge. And to be half inside and half outside such a system is to be reduced to despair. For there are two questions which still need to be asked. Is it really the case that what is called the tradition carries so clear and single a meaning? And, whatever our answer to this, what actual relations are we to see and live by, between the tradition of tragedy and the kind of experience, in our own time, that we ordinarily and perhaps mistakenly call tragic? (pp. 14–15).

We may wish to question Williams's programme for bridging tradition and modern awareness, literary and everyday experience; it should have become impossible to elude the need to bridge them. The tenacity with which he confronts this—at once academic and existential—need is perhaps the most deeply redirective achievement of his thought.

It seems to me that, in the last resort, Raymond Williams does not succeed in converting his pioneer bridges into viable reciprocities between these poles. But before I attempt to indicate the reasons for this, I am anxious to stress the enormous difficulties of the undertaking, and to acknowledge the crucial positive insights to be gained even from this ultimate failure (if such it be) to hold things steadily together. For these tensions can only be diagnosed, and lived through, by a kind of dialectical trial and error. Not only have received tragic forms been increasingly displaced in the theatre of our time; not only is our culture engaged in a progressive, systematic confusion of tragic and comic experience; the very terms in which we think about the problem—including the word tragedy itself—'slip, slide, perish,/Decay with imprecision' as our thought gropes for a foothold. In such circumstances, Williams's lucidity in posing the questions, and his struggle towards a humanism both faithful to tragic facts and truly revolutionary, will remain active powers in any further dialectic.

From the standpoint of criticism and critical theory, *Modern Tragedy* offers a range of concise, detailed responses to modern writing—always in real intimacy with their texts—forming themselves into a powerful structure of Marxist diagnosis. From the standpoint of secular humanist self-orientation, it is a plea for commitment to 'revolution'—as against tragic despair, or resignation, or absurdist 'revolt'. And, directly from the standpoint of revolutionary humanism, it is a maturely inspiring programme for seeing revolution itself essentially 'in a tragic perspective'—lest the revolutionary purpose should, under pressure, become a new form of violation, abstracted and 'set as an idea above real men' (p. 82), or lest, conversely, men failing to see revolution 'as the inevitable working through of a deep and tragic disorder' (p. 75), should, in shock and disillusion, react against 'the tragic action'—which 'in its deepest sense is not the confirmation of disorder, but its experience, its comprehension and its resolution' (p. 83).

Raymond Williams's commerce between 'tragedy' and 'revolution' vitally extends and enriches both concepts;

but I do not believe it solves either of the original problems he raises: the problem of relating traditional tragic forms to modern forms, and that of relating the tragic in art and in life.

One reason for this is simply that, in the course of his explorations, these general problems increasingly *turn into* the special issue of tragedy and revolution. Thus the correct and important insistence that tragedy is too often dogmatically sealed off from social perspectives—and that the tragic in our time must prominently include the experience of revolution—unawares slides into more and more exclusively societal determinations of tragic meanings, and especially into a tendency to equate the problem of 'modern tragedy' more and more totally with the problem of 'tragedy and revolution'. In place, then, of the promised active conjunction of past and present, of 'tragedy' and 'everyday tragedies', over the whole range of tragic experience, we arrive at a special defence of a special range of contemporary tragic significances. Inevitably, the effect of this two-fold shift, from an inclusive to a selective focus, and from one kind of partiality to another, is to leave the inclusive problem unclarified—the more so for seeming to have shifted into clarity.

We may locate the pressures towards this dislocation of focus in the procedures of *Modern Tragedy* in the underlying requirements of its vision. Especially, we shall examine in turn the following major features of the argument: (1) its overstatement of discontinuities in the tradition of literary tragedy; (2) its looseness of hold upon residual tragic necessities within the dimension of temporal redemption; and (3) —by the convergence of these preceding features—its immanent, temporal displacements of absolute, transcendent significances in tragic experience.

I TRADITION AND TRAGIC REDEMPTION

Williams prepared the ground for his programme with a review of 'tragic ideas' from classical Athens to our own time. His discussion throws a concentrated light upon every phase of literary tragedy, and poses the general questions to which we have already referred. Yet, by the end of this section, these questions have already suffered the shift we have noted. Classical and mediaeval, Renaissance and modern notions (especially those of Hegel, Schopenhauer and Nietzsche) are interrogated in relation to the problem of 'everyday tragedies'; and seen, if not actually to warrant, at any rate not to preclude, recognition of 'the tragedy of revolution' as the real legitimate offspring of 'tragic tradition' and 'everyday tragedy' in our time. Thus, what started as a firmly inclusive refusal to deny to ordinary human calamities—'a mining disaster, a burned-out family, a broken career, a smash on the road' (pp. 13–14), as well as to social convulsions like war and revolution—the dignifying title of 'tragedy', actually ushers in an increasingly constrictive conflation of 'tragic' with 'revolutionary' meanings.

This potent semantic loading for which tragedy thus becomes simply 'a response to social disorder' (p. 63) depends for its plausibility upon a prior erosion of traditional tragic meanings. It seems to me that Williams is right—and performs an important service—in insisting that 'the tradition' behind the concept of tragedy is far from carrying such a 'clear and single meaning' as is often supposed. After all, tragic art embodies tensions and developments in civilization over some 2,500 years, including the drastic passages from Greek into Christian, and Christian to secular thought-forms; while tragic theory, no less than tragic dramatic practice, necessarily reflects the special approaches and tempers of writers (like Raymond Williams himself) who have seen themselves as new pathfinders in a classic common pursuit. It is right and important to stress these creative diversities within tragic tradition, lest 'the tradition' should harden into a dead and deadening academic convention. But it is no less essential to keep in mind, to keep tasting, and re-digesting, whatever implicit coherence 'the tradition' may now embody for us, lest 'tragedy', the word, should be drained of the wine for which it is valued, to make it receptive of an altogether new substance, claiming the traditional virtues and privileges. Why, after all, if not because this classic long harvest is felt to be irreplaceably precious, should those 'half inside and half outside such a system...be reduced to despair'? Why should it be more than a verbal pedantry whether the 'long revolution' can assimilate 'tragedy', the word? It is not sufficient to say:

We are not looking for a new universal meaning of tragedy. We are looking for the structure of tragedy in our own culture (p. 62).

The problem is to achieve more than a verbal connection between 'the structure of tragedy in our own culture' and the 'universal meaning'—however complex, however elusive—in virtue of which an apparently merely verbal puzzle can threaten 'despair'.

The main tendency of Williams's critique of 'the tradition' is, however, to highlight—and, I believe, to overstate—existing divergences within it, in the interests of claiming a corresponding licence for his own programme. Thus his challenge to the assumption of a 'common' cultural form as between Greek and Elizabethan tragedy involves both an over-emphasis upon Elizabethan secularism and a strangely arrived-at undervaluing of the mediaeval tragic achievements that link them. Basing himself mainly on Chaucer's definitions in the *Monk's Tale* and its *Prologue*—and Lydgate's

> It begynneth in prosperite
> And endeth ever in adversite
> And it also doth the conquest trete
> Of riche kynges and of lordys grete

—Williams concludes that mediaeval tragedy is radically at odds with the Greek inheritance. Wheras in Greek tragedy rank was 'at once public and metaphysical'—'an involving and representative eminence', so that 'the action embodies a whole view of life' (p. 22)—the mediaeval concern with Fortune or 'worldly condition' was narrowly restricted to princely anecdotes, largely irrelevant to life as a whole:

The effect of mediaeval tragedy, then, within what was doubtless felt as a continuity, was paradoxical. It was a drastic limitation of range, and an exclusion of conflict, under the pressures of what must be seen as the alienation of feudal society. The stress on a general condition became so attached to a single particular case—the fall of princes—that the general reference became largely negative: an abstraction defining a limited action (p. 23).

Now, even within Williams's own range of references, is there, after all, such an essential break of direction between the *Monk's Tale's* emphasis:

> For certain, whan that Fortune list to flee,
> Ther may no man the cours of hire witholde.
> Lat no man truste on blynde prosperitee

and the final Chorus of *Oedipus*?:

Sons and daughters of Thebes, behold, this was Oedipus,
Greatest of men; he held the key to the deepest mysteries;
Was envied by all his fellow-men for his great prosperity;
Behold, what a full tide of misfortune swept over his head.
Then learn that mortal man must always look to his ending.
And none can be called happy until that day when he carries
His happiness down to the grave in peace.

But since not only mediaeval theory but also its practice is in view here, one can hardly fail to ask how the Mystery Cycles (does their action not embody both immediate tragic perceptions and 'a whole way of life'?) fit into this picture? Or, for that matter, the indubitably 'representative' conflicts of *Everyman*? Williams, extraordinarily, does not mention the Mystery Cycles at all; while of *Everyman* he says that, since to pass through death is not only inevitable, but the only way in which Everyman can come to his Father, 'the later tragic voice cannot come.[1] When it does come, it is unmistakable: a man alone in his extremity' (p. 89). But if Everyman's reduction to mortal aloneness seems insufficiently extreme, what of the voice that narrates the condition of Francesca da Rimini—or of Dante's enacted response: 'so that I fainted with pity, as if I had been dying; and fell as a dead body falls'? And can the mediaeval contribution to tragedy be soundly generalized without noting, in Chaucer himself, not merely the perfunctory omnium gatherum of the *Monk's Tale*, but *Troilus and Criseyde*—that humane, tragic appreciation 'that humanity is not self-sufficing'[2]—or, further afield, the romance of *Tristan and Iseult*, which, according to Denis de Rougemont, activated the fatal equation of love and the death-wish, not only in mediaeval chivalry, but, with the cumulative potency of myth, throughout the subsequent stages of our civilization?[3] The judgment that the effect of mediaeval tragedy is that of 'a drastic limitation of range, and an exclusion of conflict' under pressures whereby 'the general reference became largely negative', and lacking in metaphysical import, surely needs drastic qualification.

Similar serious question-marks have to be placed against other elements in Williams's account of 'the tradition'. Thus he maintains that 'the increasing secularization' to be found in neo-classical tragedy is reflected in 'an increasingly isolated interpretation of the character of the

---

[1] It may be significant that even this qualifying 'later' seems an afterthought; it does not occur in the original version of the essay (*New Left Review*, no. 20, Summer 1963, p. 55).

[2] John Speirs, *Chaucer the Maker*, London, 1951, p. 80.

[3] Denis de Rougemont, *Passion and Society*, London, 1940.

hero' and that 'the moving force of tragedy was now quite clearly a matter of behaviour, rather than either a metaphysical condition or a metaphysical fault' (p. 26). No doubt, this is true of Dryden, to whom he refers, but could anything be further from the real centre of gravity of neo-classical tragedy, the achieved tragic creativeness of Racine, whom Williams does not mention? A critique of tragic tradition that, omitting to take cognizance of *Phèdre* and *Athalie*, sees the moving force of tragedy at that stage as 'quite clearly' *not* 'a metaphysical condition or a metaphysical fault' may help to open the way towards a complementary present-day secularization—towards an idea of tragedy simply as 'a response to social disorder'— but only at the cost of a critical and metaphysical removal from the relevant tragic centralities.

The tendency of Williams's approach can, however, perhaps, be most clearly grasped through his comments on 'liberal tragedy'—especially as exemplified in his treatment of Ibsen's *Brand*. There are some pertinent differences between Williams's analysis of *Brand* in his *Drama from Ibsen to Eliot* (1952) and his handling of it in *Modern Tragedy*. The former, while noting the importance of social themes in *Brand*, accurately fastens upon its metaphysical vision as the governing dimension of the play. It is, he says, 'essentially a statement of the claims of vocation; and its significant conclusion is the impossibility of fulfilling the vocation of the ideal under "the load of inherited spiritual debt"'. Brand's mission is 'the restoration of wholeness', but although the call is absolute, so are the barriers. 'This tension is the whole action of the play.' Thus, whereas 'in the beginning, most of Brand's speeches are in specifically social terms...it is part of the design of the play that this emphasis should change, that the vocation should come to be defined, not as social reform, but the realisation of the actual self.' And self-realization, through the realization of his divine tasks, is limited by 'debt'—a personal liability to hereditary guilt 'which epitomizes original sin'. Only death releases the powers of mercy and love. 'It is, as Ibsen sees it, the essential tragedy of the human situation.'[1]

Williams does not repudiate this reading in his later account in *Modern Tragedy*; but there is now a framework of revolutionary theory and, going with it, a drastic contraction, and shift, of focus. *Brand* is now seen as a paradigm of 'liberal tragedy'—which arises at those points of modern awareness where difficulty and disillusion seem to show the impossibility of man's transforming his disordered existence. Thus, in its naturalist forms—corresponding to utilitarian and Fabian meliorism—liberal tragedy enacts a mechanistic conception of man, wherein suffering is merely passive, and wherein a sort of manipulated 'evolution' displaces revolution as the model of social change. In its Romantic forms, a more radical alienation in the face of unfulfilled revolutionary desires leads increasingly to a total writing off of the social world; so that man 'on the run from himself'—unable to find 'a home in the world'—is deadlocked in 'a desire that is beyond all relationships' (pp. 94–5), and 'even what begins as social criticism tends to pass into nihilism' (p. 71).

[1] *Drama from Ibsen to Eliot*, London, 1952, pp. 51–6.

Yet also there is, by the time of Ibsen's maturity, an 'increasingly confident identification of a false society as man's real enemy; the naming, in social terms, of the formerly nameless alienation' (p. 95). In *Brand*, aspiration and alienation are brought together in a necessary—and necessarily unavailing—struggle against this disordered order. For the aspiring individual cannot escape from his own shared inheritance of sickness and compromise. 'There is no way out, there is only an inevitable tragic consciousness, while desire is seen as essentially individual' (p. 100).

While desire is seen as essentially individual. In this new, explanatory perspective, the essentially theological action of *Brand* is seen in essentially secular terms; so that the way has been opened to a direct assimilation of *Brand* to a post-theological 'liberal tragedy', both in Ibsen himself and in subsequent modern drama—and so also towards Williams's own passage from 'liberal tragedy' to its secular-socialist successor. Just and illuminating as much of this is—in its detailed textual pointers, as in the conceptual framework it helps to define—there are limits to its critical reach. Thus, the effect of such a reading is to suppress the decisive metaphysical tensions generated between *Brand* and *Ghosts, The Wild Duck, Rosmersholm* and *When We Dead Awaken*, levelling them, one and all, to a uniform secular significance. The specifically theological pulse-beat of *Brand* comes to appear as little more than an epiphenomenon of the liberal deadlock; 'the impossibility of finding a home in the world' (a primary source of Shakespearean tragedy and Racine's—and indeed of much classical tragedy) is seen simply as a symptom of Romantic alienation; and even an incidental reference to Prometheus and Faust as heroes of Romantic rebellion does not register the depth of historical and metaphysical continuity this implies, but is merely related back to the 'contradictions' of 'bourgeois tragedy' (pp. 94–5).

The tendency, then, of Raymond Williams's account of 'the tradition' is to stretch its certainly important variations and transformations into essential discontinuities and disjunctions, and to tilt the balance heavily towards essentially secular emphases, even where specifically religious themes come into view. Speaking of the eighteenth century bourgeois tragedians, Williams notes an 'important loss...of dimension and reference' in their private humanitarianism. 'For the sources of tragedy were not, even in their experience, *only* private.' Pity and sympathy have, thus, little effective power in the face of crimes against property in Lillo's *The London Merchant*. 'Distress accompanies execution, and humanitarianism is at its limits...What we then see, behind the loss of dimension, is a complacent affirmation of the existing social framework' (p. 93). A fair diagnosis. But the observation may be adapted to sum up the loss of dimension and reference in Williams's own emergent tragic perspective. For the sources of the tradition he surveys were, equally, not *only* secular-social. And the tendency of a purely secular tragedy of revolution can be seen in Williams's new-model tragedy, *Koba*, where distress accompanies the most 'superhuman inhumanities' (as Wilfred Owen wrote in another context), and humanism is at its limits. Behind *this* loss of dimension and metaphysical reference we can hardly avoid seeing, though certainly no complacent reaffirmation of Stalinist inordinacies, at any rate a distressed acceptance of their immanent tragic validity. The erosion of continuities defining the dimension of tragedy is indeed no mere academic exercise.

Secularized eschatology

Raymond Williams's deepest, most central concern in his reassessments of tragedy is to affirm an inescapable unity between man's experienced tragic existence and his imperative self-liberation. Potentially, at least, 'the whole action' of tragedy (pp. 82, 242) is always, for him, more than the immediate disaster or deadlock: a stage in the process of human self-redemption. Conversely, he insists, it behoves us to take the weight of the cost, the real, human—past or present—cost of whatever degree of liberation is being reaped. To acquiesce in history's tragic disorders—whether in despair, or resignation, or hopeless 'revolt'—is to fail our human potentialities of redemption. But, equally, to repress, or disown, our direct humane reactions against principled inhumanity amidst the redemptive 'necessities' of revolution is merely to transmit in new forms these alienating disorders—although these new evils are subject in their turn to redemptive transformation; so that the ultimate 'whole action'—the ultimate wholeness of the 'long revolution'—can yet endow even such newly emerging evils with an ultimate tragic validity.

The mature complexity of this poise, and the radical

integrity of its demands, raise Williams's work to a classic stature. Despite its evident perils—which Williams does not always succeed in negotiating—his very personal fusion of Marxist and literary insights releases decisive powers of humaneness, which we shall do well to safeguard and extend. It is just because of this pathfinding importance that *Modern Tragedy* requires our most alert critical caution as we make our own what claims us among its perceptions and demands.

It seems to me that there are some crucial infirmities in Williams's vision of evil and tragic redemption—closely related to the treatment of tragic tradition we have been considering. Like Marx himself, Raymond Williams employs the religious concept of 'redemption' to define an absolute dimension of human hope, absolutely free of any transcendent reference. Thus he gives great prominence to Marx's early conception of revolution, as stated in his *Zur Kritik der Hegelschen Rechts-Philosophie*:

A class must be formed which has *radical chains*, a class in civil society which is not a class of civil society, a class which is the dissolution of all classes, a sphere of society which has a universal character because its sufferings are universal, and which does not claim a *particular redress* because the wrong which is done to it is not a *particular wrong* but *wrong in general*. There must be formed a sphere of society which claims no *traditional* status but only a *human* status...a sphere finally which cannot emancipate itself without emancipating itself from all other spheres of society, without therefore emancipating all these other spheres; which is, in short, a *total loss* of humanity and which can only redeem itself by a *total redemption of humanity*.

'So absolute a conception', Williams comments, 'distinguishes revolution from rebellion, or, to put it another way, makes political revolution into a general human revolution' (p. 76). But here Williams's revolutionary optimism fuses with his tragic vision: 'This idea of "the total redemption of humanity" has the ultimate cast of resolution and order, but in the real world its perspective is inescapably tragic' (p. 77).

But then I do not believe, as so many disillusioned or broken by actual revolution have come to believe, that the suffering can be laid to the charge of the revolution alone, and that we must avoid revolution if we are to avoid suffering. On the contrary, I see revolution as the inevitable working through of a deep and tragic disorder, to which we can respond in varying ways but which will in any case, in one way or another, work its way through our world, as a consequence of any of our actions. I see revolution, that is to say, in a tragic perspective...Marx's early idea of revolution seems to me to be tragic in this sense (p. 75).

The question, however, imposes itself how 'so *absolute* a conception' of 'the *total* redemption of humanity'—having 'the *ultimate* cast of resolution and order' about it—can come to inhere solely within the relativities, and limits, and necessary contingencies of human time.

It is only necessary to attend to this question to see it as—on the face of it—indicating a strict, logical impossibility. *Either*, it seems, these quasi-eschatological notions must therefore be seen as loosely focused metaphors—whose literal significance would need to be re-investigated from scratch—*or* they must be restored to a strictly eschatological context. One of the achievements of

Williams's work is to bring this dilemma, inherent in any messianic secularism, to a sort of phenomenological test—beyond verbal logicalities: the evidences of the tragic imagination. Too often revolutionary humanists have been unwilling, or unable, to lay themselves open to such a test. There are always immediate realizable urgencies, tangible motivating objectives, to attend to; and, beyond these, a secularized eschatology of redemption virtually taboo from concrete, critical penetration. *Modern Tragedy* goes further towards meeting these problems than any previous enquiry.

But how far does it achieve a viable resolution of these problems? We have stressed the *prima facie* conflict, in verbal logic, between the absolutes of secular redemption and the inherent limitations of secular contingencies. Williams, however, neither elects to assimilate 'total redemption' to a kingdom beyond all time, nor to turn back, critically, upon these quasi-eschatological terms. Instead, he concentrates upon exposing himself, stoically and without blinking, to the reality of the difficulties, and the inevitable long-term duration, of the revolutionary process itself—and thence to assimilating 'the long revolution' to 'the whole action' of tragedy:

And all our experience tells us that this complicated action between real men will continue as far ahead as we can foresee, and that the suffering in this continuing struggle will go on being terrible. It is very difficult for the mind to accept this, and we all erect our defences against so tragic a recognition. But I believe that it is inevitable, and that we must speak of it if it is not to overwhelm us (p. 78).

But how far ahead—*sub specie temporis*—is 'as far ahead as we can foresee'? Indeed is so 'inevitable' and 'tragic a recognition' tolerant of any conceptual assimilation to 'total redemption' at all? There are times when the ultimate fullness of revolution seems hardly more than an image, abstracted, like Brecht's St Neverneverday, from the terrible beauty of living revolutions.[1] Can the mind properly accept such an indeterminate finality, such an infinitely receding 'future', at all, as pertinent to the tragic, moral actuality—here and now—of 'the price of the future, the heavy but necessary price' (p. 255: *Koba*)? It is not for nothing that 'the whole action' of tragedy is classically defined by an actually enacted beginning, middle and end. Such is not only a purely destructive action like that of *Hippolytus*; but tragic redemption, too, has traditionally always been either a process of finite timely achievements (like the emergence of civilized justice in the *Oresteia*) or of an absolute, transcendent salvation, finally at home beyond temporal limits (as in *Lear* and *Brand*). A conception of tragic 'redemption' which is neither a definite, finite historical process, nor a consummating infinity, for which history is only a

[1] Compare the passage just cited with, for instance: 'We have still to attend to the whole action, and to see liberation as part of the same process as the terror which appals us. I do not mean that the liberation cancels the terror; I mean only that they are connected, and that this connection is tragic. The final truth in this matter seems to be that revolution—the long revolution against human alienation—produces, in real historical circumstances, its own new kinds of alienation, which it must struggle to understand, and which it must overcome, if it is to remain revolutionary' (p. 82). ('Overcome'—once and for all; or producing its own, new kinds of alienation 'as far ahead as we can foresee?')

beginning (and middle), cannot but be at odds with itself: it either claims too little or too much.

It is too late, in the perspectives of our decade—at any rate for a mind of Williams's resolute openness to the facts—to return to simpler, more determinate historical blueprints. Is there, then, any escape from these revolutionary contradictions if not either in some active socio-religious eschatology, or, alternatively, an active recognition that 'the total redemption of humanity' is merely a hyperbolic metaphor of limited historical hopes? How, after all, is one to understand a foreseen 'total' historical achievement, foreseen as remaining unachieved for 'as far ahead as we can foresee?'

Nevertheless, Williams declines either to name this total redemption of humanity as the fulfilment of the kingdom of God, or to retreat into less absolute—so to speak demythologized—revolutionary expectations. He merely insists that the long revolution is long indeed, and that, so long as 'the whole action' remains unfinished, its tragic course will have 'the ultimate cast of resolution and order', though not—not yet—the fullness of resolution and order, not yet the totality of human redemption. Not yet; and yet the totality of human redemption is totally a matter of history—and totally within the gift of men's own action in history. The evils of human existence, however enormous, are only fragments of history. And history—in travail for its ultimate mastery by men—must itself be the source, and arena, of their ultimate, total redemption.

Tradition and Tragic Redemption

Evil in history

It is in the conception of evil requisite for such a notion of redemption that revolutionary theory and the tragic imagination confront each other most sharply. And it is here that Williams, the literary critic, brings his commitments as revolutionary thinker most decisively to the test of the dramatized phenomenology of tragic art. If the fullness of revolution—however, whenever achieved—by definition involves bringing down the curtain on tragic existence, then the evils men suffer or inflict within our present, tragic dispensation, must be fully avoidable on the far side of revolution. However inevitable, however stringently 'fated', a given tragic pattern may seem—or indeed be—within past or present historical contexts, such tragic 'necessities' are necessary only relative to these contexts; they belong to the legion of symptoms of human self-estrangement which is to be remedied by revolution. There are no 'absolute' or 'transcendent' evils, no irreparable patterns of fatality, no historically irresolvable forms of catastrophe or affliction. Our widespread, ingrained assumptions to the contrary are rooted not in the facts but in ideology—that very ideology which orthodox modern tragedy and tragic theory since Schopenhauer and Nietzsche have been enacting with such completeness that it is hard to place oneself sufficiently outside its spell to recognize it as ideological—as merely a direct, conditioned reflection of a pre-revolutionary anguish and impotence.

Williams presses this argument with extraordinary

resourcefulness, and a deeply disciplined humanist passion. Time and again he turns the tables on us as we prepare to counter his tragic optimism (with those very reflexes of conditioned alienation he is at pains to lay bare and re-train) by bringing into play his own thorough awareness of the depth and complexity of the evils to be surmounted. Above all, his literary analyses bring home the close integration of theory and immediate human responsiveness in his vision; and while he knows, and insists upon, the connections between social and private evils, he also knows how elusively indirect these connections can be, and is under no illusion that human anguish can be exorcised simply by revolutionary decree.

Nevertheless, what he proves is less—much less—than he needs to prove; though he makes decisive inroads into current conventional pessimism and reactionary rationales for social passivity. The ultimate requirements of his vision can be gauged not only from his insistent denials of what he calls 'the mask of Fate' (p. 180)—of tragedy as somehow 'inherent' in the human situation (p. 106), of tragic evil as some sort of 'absolute condition' (pp. 59, 181)—but, more positively, from such pointers as his comments upon eighteenth century 'poetic justice':

Tragedy, in this view, shows suffering as a consequence of error, and happiness as a consequence of virtue...That is to say, the bad will suffer and the good will be happy; or rather, much as in the medieval emphasis, the bad will do badly in the world, and the good will prosper. The moral impetus of tragedy is then the realisation of this kind of consequence. The spectator will be moved to live well by the demonstration of the consequences of good and evil. And, further, within the action itself, the characters themselves will be capable of the same recognition and change. Thus the tragic catastrophe either moves its spectators to moral recognition and resolution, or can be avoided altogether, by a change of heart.

It is customary, now, to condescend to this view, and to assume its inevitable shallowness. But what was weak in it was not the underlying demand, which is indeed inevitable, but its inability to conceive morality as other than static (p. 31).

In other words, the only real objection to this view —which assumes an exhaustively explanatory connection between tragic affliction and moral failure—lies in the inadequacy of its concrete moral background. The implication is that, in principle (given an adequate, revolutionary morality) there really is no type of human suffering that is not either capable of 'resolution' or of being 'avoided altogether'. We could almost say that for Raymond Williams 'the total redemption of humanity' is, precisely, the ultimate 'poetic justice'—a poetry to be made flesh in history by our capacity for 'recognition and change'.

Even, however, on the plane of social relations as such, that other human capacity, for changing from order to disorder, from 'being' into 'having', from community into alienation, must remain a permanent threat to poetic justice in history, since history is written in moral prose. This, of course, is no argument for depreciating, or despairing of, the imperative historical drive towards justice and real community. Indeed, Williams himself comes very close, as we saw, not only to recognizing that 'in real historical circumstances' the long revolution itself produces 'new kinds of alienation', but that 'this complicated action between real men will continue as far ahead as we can foresee, and that the suffering in this continuing struggle will go on being terrible'. It is just that this deeply ascetic factual recognition must somehow be brought to bear upon the imagery of 'total redemption' if this poetry is to belong not to 'fancy' but the 'imagination'—if both our human rootedness in tragedy and the divinity that shapes our total redemptive hopes are to be recognized for what they are.

Self-redemption

The problem is not solved by a human appropriation of divine titles, any more than by the secularization of eschatological terms. There is a great deal of talk in *Koba* about 'man the creator' (pp. 235, 274), about men 'who cannot be mastered' (pp. 22 ff.), about being 'more than men, not less' (p. 233). But while Max (the play's Trotsky-figure) goes so far as to say:

It is God, surely? It is man as god. To create from chaos, having first created himself—

Jordan (Lenin) gives warning that 'man the creator, the towering figure on the crest of the hill', can

fall like a statue, the fists clenched in stone and the arms rigid in dignity; unable, at last, even to reach out and save himself, reach out and break his fall (p. 235).

The immediate reference is of course to Stalin—we think of the pictures of razed statues of 1956—but the ultimate implications are much more far-reaching. Indeed, they may reach further than Williams had in mind—not merely directing us to the 'long revolution' (a new, youthful, revisionist 'Joseph' appears—an equivocal omen—at the end of the play) but returning us sharply to the problem of man's total self-redemption.

The danger is—and metaphysics apart, as *Koba* and its historical sources show, there are also serious *moral* dangers —that a totally self-redemptive reaching for Godot is merely the converse of waiting for him in total self-estrangement. This is as true, though of course in different ways, of revolutionary divinization as of the sexual absolutes of Lawrentian private salvation. The image of Godot lurks—a merciless chaos of infinity and limit— behind both types of man-made redemption. For man, as man, is finally subject to limit; not least in his absolute need of redemptive divinization. For men are men, and can fail; and, even where they succeed, are subject to failure—and death. Man the creator *and* man the corrupter, human community *and* disablement from communion—the grandeur *and* misery of man—groan for perfections beyond human resources. It is radically necessary to man to transcend these resources; and tragically beyond him to transcend them. Beyond any given, redeemable human failure, there is always the grave, constant option of revolution; but beyond the redeeming Absolute with whom Job wrestled—and Christ, at the moment of death—there is finally only Godot.

The return to Lawrence and Beckett, in this context, is not arbitrary. For it seems to me that D. H. Lawrence's dedicated pursuit of an absolute totality in personal relations and the pursuit of a revolutionary, total communal redemption are the complementary growing-points of modern humanism; and that both, at one and the same time, tower prophetically above the jaded pusillanimities of liberal pragmatism—and Establishment Christianity—and fail to come to terms with the inescapable limits of their own heroic visions. Both, moreover, are mutually aware that private and social relations are complementary and interdependent. And both meet their ultimate, indestructible challenge in the massive, multiple dead-end of Samuel Beckett.

It is not that Beckett's is the ultimate truth. Beckett's vision is no less partial, in its claims to a final universality, than theirs; and indeed if (impossibly) the choice were simply a choice between Lawrentian and Marxist commitments on the one hand and Beckett's stasis of anguish on the other, I should choose to adhere to the former—if only in the name of primitive human imperatives. But of course our real choice is not of this kind. The confrontation is anything but simple. The challenge cuts both ways. Lawrence fails to reckon with inescapable irreducible human failure—or rather, in the end he refuses to *care* about such lives; while Beckett, conversely, refuses, or is unable, to recognize life's openness to real fruition. Raymond Williams is as deeply aware of the realities of human fruition as of radical failure and anguish—and affirms the ultimate hope of a total communal redemption; Beckett not only acknowledges no such communal hope but insists that, in any case, radical personal outrage must remain for ever unredeemed in the absence of personal salvation. Each of these visions safeguards essential human truths. So does the tension between them. We cannot, without violence to human integrity and human vocation, disown any of these perspectives. Yet they also seem truly exclusive—indestructibly in contradiction. Between them, they map out—in necessary, shifting interaction—the ultimate reaches and limits, and inherent contradictions, of post-Christian humanist bearings.

II REDEMPTION AND REVOLUTION

Raymond Williams strives to unite fidelity to tragic realities with an absolute secular revolutionary faith. On the social plane this leads him, as we have seen, to a highly problematic, indefinitely recessive, conception of 'total redemption'—and to attendant moral risks. And, so long as 'so absolute a conception[1] of some actual social future is envisaged, it is proper to ask how much is included in this conceptual absoluteness. There is a story about a conference of French writers, soon after the last war, in which a Marxist, discussing the mastery of human suffering under socialism, was asked what he thought of the problem of, for instance, a child run over in a traffic accident. His reply was that, in a truly socialist society, there would be no traffic accidents. It is not necessary to approach these problems with a similar ingenuousness in order to recognize the pertinence of such simple questions. Social injustices aside—and can we really envisage an era when *all* injustice and alienation will belong to the past?—accidents will never be wholly avoidable (at any rate, there

[1] Cf. p. 199, above.

will always be floods and earthquakes). It surely cannot be mere pedantry, or paralysis, that continues to find such problems to the point.

Evil and 'total redemption'

There would of course be no such problem if the theoretic future were not called upon to redress past and present actualities so absolutely. But in that case the whole imaginative universe of the 'total redemption of humanity' by revolution—and the whole moral calculus going with it—would wither away. Nor is this 'total redemption' limited to social relations and the externals of man's control of his destiny. The hope extends essentially to the whole of men's lives—and deaths. Death—as Jan Kott notes, à propos of *King Lear*, quoting Ionesco's *Tueur sans Gages*—is the ultimate alienation: 'We shall all die, this is the only serious alienation'.[1] Raymond Williams, however, insists not only that, in principle, human life can wholly surpass 'the mask of Fate', but that even the ultimate givenness of death is wholly redeemable: in our own pulses.

It is here that Williams's tendency, which we have examined at some length, to elude traditional tragic bearings whilst continuing to lay claim to traditional tragic resonances, and his tendency to identify 'everyday tragedies' in modern experience more and more totally with remediable social disorders, impinge most critically upon the evidences of literary tragedy. Indeed, there is a decisive gap between some of Williams's own insights into the

[1] Jan Kott, *Shakespeare our Contemporary*, London, 1964, p. 123.

relevant modern literature and his concern to peel away 'the mask of Fate' from every kind of human waste to reveal an underlying remediable disorder.

Many of his most central literary analyses thus converge towards a demonstration of the condition of post-liberal 'stalemate', emerging out of the liberal 'deadlock':

In a deadlock, there is still effort and struggle, but no possibility of winning: the wrestler with life dies as he gives his last strength. In a stalemate, there is no possibility of movement or even the effort of movement; every willed action is self-cancelling. A different structure of feeling is then initiated:... the victim turning on himself (p. 142).

This conception is brilliantly applied to Chekhov and Pirandello, Eliot and even Camus; and much else in modern writing is illuminated by it. The resulting critical enrichment and sharpening of our general modern picture still need, however, to be related to Williams's controlling idea of *totally particular* historical disorders and—so also—the prospect of a *total* historical redemption. But at this most critical point of contact between revolutionary aspirations and tragic phenomena, *Modern Tragedy* slides decisively into overstatement.

Thus it is not only society's 'incorporation of all its people, *as whole human beings*' (p. 76—original italics) that the long revolution is to achieve, but liberation—or at least potential liberation—from every type of alleged 'absolute or transcendent' evil (p. 59), personal as well as social. Williams is much less explicit about the personal implications of this vision than about its social ends, and this makes it very difficult to grasp the full, concrete meaning of 'the total redemption of humanity' in Williams's borrowing. But, though he hardly specifies the horizons, or depth, or manner of personal redemption to be envisaged, there is a pervasive, resolute rejection of evil 'as inescapable and irreparable' (p. 59)—of tragedy as, in any sense, 'inherent' (p. 106) in the human condition as such. The intensity with which any such 'absolute' tragic notions are rejected fuses with his insistence that tragedy and 'everyday tragedies' must be seen as related, and that the tragic is not merely something that happens (something we merely take in, like spectators) but something that makes demands on us: demands to redeem. The impulse is deeply humane—bordering on an essentially religious humaneness—but, in this form, embodies serious confusions.

These confusions are partly factual, partly logical, and involve some corresponding semantic shifts. On the factual plane, there is an overstatement of the distinguishing tendencies of 'modern tragedy'—to the point of attributing to the drama of liberal 'deadlock' and 'stalemate' a historical singularity not borne out by the evidences of tragic literature as a whole. It is true that modern writing has tended to fashion these patterns into an orthodoxy, but they have not sprung, fully armed, from the head of the modern liberal predicament. The 'wrestler with life' who—like Brand—'dies as he gives his last strength', with 'no possibility of winning', after all has an ancestry reaching back as far as Antigone, and which includes not only Cordelia and—very differently—Dr Faustus, but perhaps also Tristan and Phèdre (and certainly

includes every historical martyrdom in the face of unequal historical odds). Similarly, the condition of 'stalemate'—'the victim turning on himself'—cannot be simply
equated with 'the final crisis of individualism, beyond the
heroic deadlock of liberal tragedy' (p. 151), but has its
classical prototype in Hamlet—followed by the 'comic'
sentimental education of *Le Misanthrope*, Swiftian self-
laceration, and so to Werther, the *Ode to a Nightingale*
and the encroaching waste land. It would seem, then,
that Raymond Williams's conclusion 'that what is now
offered as a total meaning of tragedy is in fact a particular
meaning, to be understood and valued historically' (p. 61),
only holds if the terms 'particular' and 'historically' are
stretched to allow for essential structural analogies comprehending not merely the 'deadlocks' and 'stalemates'
peculiar to our age but their deep historical roots in tragic
tradition.

'Temporary' and 'permanent' evils

Once the sense of tragedy as 'inherent' and 'inescapable'
in human existence has been diagnosed as, substantially,
a peculiarity of our time, the ground is prepared for
concluding that 'tragic necessity' is a merely relative
phenomenon—which may, thus, be totally surmounted
in the future. One more step, however, is needed for
such a conclusion: to show that the notion of tragedy as
'a total condition' (p. 179) is not only relative in the
sense of attaching peculiarly to the age of liberal deadlock and stalemate (and I have suggested that it is in fact a
deeply traditional notion) but is, indeed, an intrinsic

falsification of false perspective. Williams offers to show this in the context of his critique of Camus, whom he charges with a 'refusal of history'—or, as Sartre has put it, 'a bitter wisdom which seeks to deny time':

Camus seems, again and again, to take an historical action, and to draw much of his feeling from it, only to put it, in the end, outside history (p. 184).

Thus, in *Cross Purpose* (*Le Malentendu*):

The voice speaks of pity and kindness, but the action speaks of fate, an indifferent, arbitrary and tragic fate. And we have to ask (Camus would have insisted on asking) what are the sources of this perceived condition, especially when it is asserted as common. There is an ambiguity, an honest ambiguity, at the centre of Camus's work, for he recognises the sources of this condition in particular circumstances, and yet also asserts that it is absolute (p. 179).

This 'ambiguity'—asserting the absoluteness of particular circumstances, identifying particular historical conditions with 'fate'—is the locus of radical ultimate evasions—of a 'false consciousness'. For thus the demands for historical revolution are smothered, and displaced by 'a metaphysical revolt against an eternal injustice'—which can far too easily warrant a sort of resigned complicity with concrete historical evils. And so the 'mask of Fate' is both factually and morally falsifying.

As a critique of absurdist politics this surely drives home —though Camus's insistent concern with the morality of means remains correspondingly relevant to the politics of revolution.[1] But metaphysically, despite its initial

[1] I have entered more fully into this dilemma of the relations between 'the morality of means' and 'the politics of revolution' in a paper

plausibility, the critique ultimately backfires. For where, at the level of tragic metaphysics, does evasion finally lie: in the acknowledgement of 'permanent contradictions' (p. 175) in man's condition, or in an assertion of their total historical solubility?

'The ambiguity' that sees particular tragic circumstances as, at the same time, rooted in an 'absolute' condition certainly is no evidence in itself of a sleight of vision. Obviously, any human experience at all, within history, is—whatever ultimate meanings it may have, or not have—'particular' and 'historical'. Williams repeatedly seems to imply (in his treatment of Strindberg, Pirandello, and Eliot, as well as Camus) that to show that a writer's tragic vision relates to concrete particulars of time and place is, *ipso facto*, to show that any sense of 'permanent' or 'absolute' meanings inherent in these must be illusory or evasive. Only a positivist empiricism (such as was buried by Wittgenstein) could, with consistency, deploy such a logic; it is especially disconcerting to come upon traces of it in the hands of so Hegelian a writer as Raymond Williams.

Everything depends upon the actual nature—the phenomenological structure—of the particulars at issue. And Camus, like Strindberg or Pirandello, is after all at pains to analyse these structures of consciousness—and their sources in human facts—and they all advance positive grounds for their various tragic assertions of 'permanent contradictions' in human existence. These assertions, and

included in *From Culture to Revolution*, edited by Terry Eagleton and Brian Wicker, London, 1968.

the grounds advanced on their behalf, are unequal in force: some are unsubstantiated or clearly unsound, some dubious—and some surely irresistible, once they have been allowed to penetrate us. To distinguish, with careful particularity, between such resonances is one of the main tasks of tragic criticism—and an essential critical basis of tragic theory.

There is very little attempt in *Modern Tragedy* to go into such distinctions. A case is established against O'Neill and Tennessee Williams, of 'a false particularity'—that is, of imposing from the outside 'the characteristic metaphysics of the isolate' (pp. 118–19). And one must agree that 'it is as easy to relate' the 'social world of temporary relationships, transience and bright emptiness' of Eliot's *Cocktail Party* 'to the particular place and the people as to a common human condition' (p. 164). But the great tragic constants of human blindness or perception, failure to meet or falls from communication, need of what cannot be or loss of the utterly needed—already endemic in Sophocles and Shakespeare and Racine—cannot be generalized away into mere particularities of situation or history.

Williams's argument hardly comes to grips with such tragic universals, or their bearings upon the concept of the 'total redemption of humanity'. For the most part, the argument merely relies upon a strong general emphasis on the 'particular circumstances' of tragedy, together with a similar general stress upon history as a transformer of circumstances. So, in the concluding essay —on Brecht:

We have to see not only that suffering is avoidable, but that it is not avoided. And not only that suffering breaks us, but that it need not break us. Brecht's own words are the precise expression of this new sense of tragedy:

The sufferings of this man appal me, because they are unnecessary.

This feeling extends into a general position: the new tragic consciousness of all those who, appalled by the present, are *for this reason* firmly committed to a different future: to the struggle against suffering learned in suffering: a total exposure which is also a total involvement (pp. 202–3).

Yes—indeed. Yes, yes; *but...*

But not every particular suffering is avoidable. The appalling struggle against suffering learned in suffering, though always redemptive, cannot always be effectively practical:

> If thou wilt weep my fortunes, take my eyes;
> I know thee well enough, thy name is Gloucester.

It may well be a struggle against necessary suffering.

Raymond Williams seems to conclude that tragic suffering is avoidable altogether, though, appallingly, it is not avoided—and not avoidable this side of revolution. And indeed, some such vision seems implicit in the concept of 'the total redemption of humanity' by revolution. There are, however, some places where Williams himself approaches a very different recognition; and it is striking that these relate to D. H. Lawrence on the one hand and Camus himself on the other. Comparing Lawrence's *Women in Love* and *Lady Chatterley's Lover* with *Anna Karenina*, Williams accuses Lawrence precisely of 'dodging' the ultimate challenge of the tragic:

Lawrence misses the decisive question: how can it be that real, potent life is necessarily destroyed by the 'morality...of life itself'? The point will be very important at a later stage of our argument. Meanwhile we can notice the prepared escape route [*Lady Chatterley's Lover*], in which the full claims of individual life are asserted, without the necessity of tragedy.

An escape route, of course, from the logic of his own position; not necessarily an escape route from life itself (p. 124).

And to Lawrence's charge against Tolstoy, of 'wetting on the flame' by allowing Anna Karenina's life to be sacrificed to 'the social code', to 'the mere judgment of man'—rather than to flow with 'the vast, uncomprehended and incomprehensible morality of nature or of life itself', the 'greater, uncomprehended morality, or fate'—Williams replies decisively:

The child of the body is there, in any society. Frustration and hatred are there, under any laws, if the relationships are wrong. The tragedy of Anna is exacerbated by her society, but the roots of the tragedy lie much deeper, in a specific relationship (just as, in contemporary societies in which the old sexual laws and conventions have been practically abandoned, men and women still kill themselves in despair of love) (p. 129).

These facts of life are decisive not only for what is at issue between Lawrence and Tolstoy, but for every kind of total commitment—including Raymond Williams's own—to a 'new sense of tragedy' totally defined by the feeling:

The sufferings of this man appal me, because they are unnecessary.

Some sufferings appal us because they are necessary; because we perceive that, in any society, in however revolutionized a future, such sufferings will persist; because we sense, within them, or beyond them, an uncomprehended and incomprehensible morality—or *anti*-morality—or fate; because we glimpse that, since the roots of such sufferings lie much deeper than any social injustice, only on St Neverneverday—or at the Last Judgment—will a poetic justice reign; because 'the total redemption of humanity' seems both necessary and impossible—fatefully usurped by specific tragic necessities.

It is surely remarkable that Raymond Williams—the theorist of total redemption by revolution—should recognize, in the mirror of Lawrence—the poet of total self-fulfilment—those limits to human self-redemption which *both* these forms of heroic aspiration are totally committed to surpassing. (Samuel Beckett's insistences lie in wait for them both.) Frustration and hatred are there, under any laws, if the relationships are wrong—and there will always be specifically wrong relationships. For the most part, Raymond Williams's critical and theoretical judgments by-pass, or emphatically deny, this recognition. Thus, to question, as he does, 'the fact of evil as inescapable and irreparable' (p. 59); to say 'we cannot...say that tragedy is the recognition of transcendent evil' (p. 60); and to assert—*without qualification*—'that man is not "naturally" anything: that we both create and transcend our limits, and that we are good or evil in particular ways and in particular situations, defined by the pressures we at once receive and can alter and can create again' (p. 60)—seems to prepare an escape route not merely from particular situations and limits but an escape route from life itself.

Tolstoy and Lawrence between them should have served warning against this route. But it is only in the (penultimate) chapter on Camus that '*the permanent contradictions of life*' (p. 180) are at last explicitly acknowledged; only to give way once more, in conclusion, to the 'new sense of tragedy' for which 'suffering is avoidable'—'the new tragic consciousness of all those who, appalled by the present, are *for this reason* firmly committed to a different future'.

The momentary acknowledgment of 'the permanent contradictions of life' is so crucial to the whole concept of 'the total redemption of humanity' in history that we have to give full weight to the context in which it occurs, and to Williams's immediate inferences from it. It is evidently arrived at with great reluctance, and accorded very little stress. Indeed, as we saw, Williams's purpose is precisely to reject the conception of tragedy as 'inherent' —as 'absolute or transcendent', as 'a total condition' or unavoidable fate. And his reference to 'the permanent contradictions of life' occurs in the very course of his objections to the 'ambiguity...at the centre of Camus's work' which recognizes the sources of tragedy 'in particular circumstances, and yet also asserts that it is absolute':

It is not an evasion of the permanent contradictions of life to recognize and name a more particular and temporary contradiction. Rather, the naming of the latter as Fate is itself evasion (p. 180).

Is this not an implicit, backhanded endorsement of precisely those tragic 'names' the passage seems to disqualify? It may (or may not) be 'evasion' to 'name *a more par-*

ticular and temporary contradiction' as 'Fate'; but then, how does this bear upon '*the permanent* contradictions of life'—which, after all, are the heart of the problem? May '*the permanent contradictions of life*' be named, without evasion, as 'Fate'; or might it even seem evasive to name these 'permanent contradictions of life' *permanent contradictions (irreducible to* 'more particular and temporary contradictions')?

The radical elusiveness of the passage derives most immediately from its equivocal compression. On the face of it, its two sentences seem stably, symmetrically balanced— the former precluding, the latter affirming, a locus of evasive 'naming'. Actually, however, their relation is unstably oblique, so that no consistent statement concerning 'permanent contradictions' on the one hand, and 'particular and temporary' contradictions on the other, emerges, but an amalgam in which 'the permanent contradictions of life' (which in retrospect are equated—or *are* they?—with 'Fate') seem alternately endorsed and disowned as a properly 'nameable' source of tragedy in its own right. This is not, however, merely a matter of local loose language. The whole tendency of the argument is to shift us away from any sense of evil as 'absolute or transcendent', 'inescapable and irreparable' (p. 59), from suffering as 'inevitable' (p. 77), tragedy as 'inherent' (p. 106)—away, that is, from any sense of 'permanent contradictions' (p. 175)—towards a 'general position' that sees suffering as 'avoidable' and 'unnecessary'. So that, when it comes, the apparent acknowledgement of 'the permanent contradictions of life' surely demands a maximum of alertness and careful explication of relationship to the over-all argument. Looseness and ambiguity at this point cannot help seeming evasive—precisely in attributing evasion through ambiguity to others—the more so since very little further attention is given to the matter. Is *all* human evil and suffering 'avoidable' or not? Does 'the *total* redemption of humanity' have to reckon with '*permanent* contradictions' in life or not? Is the 'different future', to which 'the new tragic consciousness' commits us, to resolve only 'particular circumstances' that appal us or also: 'the permanent contradictions of life'?

Camus (it is a tribute to both Camus and Raymond Williams) evidently confronts Raymond Williams with the ineluctable force of 'the permanent contradictions of life'. And Williams confronts these permanent contradictions with an ineluctable necessity to contradict them. For Camus—with Beckett—represents the ultimate logic of human limits; and Williams (with Lawrence) the logic of absolute temporal aspirations. The necessary tension between these positions (since each of them embodies essential human truths) at once prescribes and precludes the total redemption of men by men; for

This is the monstruosity in love, lady, that the will is infinite, and the execution confined; that the desire is boundless, and the act a slave to limit.

But this same tension—the crucial tension of tragic experience—can also point beyond itself, towards significances that can comprehend both:

If thou wilt weep my fortunes, take my eyes;
I know thee well enough; thy name is Gloucester:
Thou must be patient; we came crying hither:
Thou know'st the first time we smell the air
We waul and cry.

Thou hast one daughter
Who redeems nature from the general curse
Which twain have brought her to.

Music, awake her: strike ! (*Music.*)
'Tis time: descend: be stone no more; approach;
Strike all that look upon with marvel. Come;
I'll fill your grave up: stir; nay, come away;
Bequeath to death your numbness, for from him
Dear life redeems you.

O Wonder !
How many goodly creatures are there here !
How beauteous mankind is ! O brave new world
That has such people in't.

III   REDEMPTION AND TRAGIC TRANSCENDENCE

The essential paradox of any redemptive secular humanism
—a humanism which recognizes the *donnés* of time's
tragedia humana, while affirming an ultimate, temporal
Comedy in the making—is that to find one's redemptive
bearings thus totally within the secular is inevitably to
cast time also as an omnipotent '*deus ex machina*'. Within
this essential paradox, we may distinguish three overlapping 'contradictions'—both logical and existential:
(*a*) between 'the permanent contradictions of life' and
a 'totally redeemed' future; (*b*) between the merely
accidental, or avoidable, or contingent, and the inescapable

absoluteness of tragic meanings; and (*c*)—a special case of both (*a*) and (*b*): their paradigm and convergence— between death as the ultimate human limit and its inescapably absolute, infinite human meaning. And, radically posed by these problems as a whole there is, finally, the problem of sheer, absurd excruciation, and of the meaning of sacrificial meanings.

It is the first of these contradictions which bears most obviously upon the problem of secular tragic redemption, and we have looked into it at length. But, though this of itself indicates the ultimate insufficiency of a purely secular concept of redemption, it is only in the remaining contradictions that this is evident in full depth. We could say that, whilst (*a*) pursues the problem mainly along the horizontal dimension of time, (*b*) and (*c*) lay hold upon it vertically. Although, in concrete experience, these are all aspects of a closely-knit 'total condition', it is under the aspects of (*b*) and (*c*) that this condition reveals its inmost nature.

Transcendent meanings

Tragic awareness is the awareness of absolute violation of being: a confrontation with infinite meanings. This is the defining distinction between 'mere suffering' and tragic awareness. The witness of tragic tradition—as of any authentic direct response to tragic exposure—is basically just this: that man is the locus of absolute violations of being. Tragedy occurs where we enter the timeless significance of such violations:

People change, and smile: but the agony abides.

Redemption and Tragic Transcendence

The agony abides beyond individual time-spans. Nothing merely in time can redeem history's tragic facts. It is not just that some of life's 'contradictions' are 'permanent', so that total temporal redemption is a permanent contradiction-in-hope; but that those many tragic facts which history can—and must—prevent from recurring, are not thereby remedied, or repaired, or redeemed. 'The sufferings of this man appal me, because they are unnecessary'; and those of that man appal me because they are necessary. Either way, we confront a timeless violation. Even the 'accidental' or—in abstraction—'unnecessary' may thus come to be charged with a sort of fateful, irreversible absoluteness:

> What might have been is an abstraction
> Remaining a perpetual possibility
> Only in a world of speculation.

This applies equally to tragic suffering and to tragic wickedness. Troilus's violated love-faith, like Hamlet's knowledge of Gertrude's 'frailty', is totally irresolvable in time. Regan and Goneril are as timeless, as moral presences in time, as the agony of:

> I know when one is dead, and when one lives.

Such significances need to be kept distinct from 'the permanent contradictions of life', though there are of course intimate convergences between them. To say that there is a 'transcendent' quality in the evil of *Macbeth* does not conflict with the final purgation of 'the present horror from the time'. It does, however, tell us something—essential to our response—about the nature of this evil, and the nature of any redemption from this evil. At last, 'the time is free'—but only at the cost of much that, in time, remains tragically irreparable; and, most tragically of all, at the cost of the eternal exclusion of Macbeth and Lady Macbeth themselves from the redemptive potency of the whole action.

In its concern to vindicate redemptive action in history, *Modern Tragedy* both overstates the scope of redemption-in-time and confuses redemptive progress in time with reparation, or redemption, of what time is for ever loaded with,

> Like the river with its cargo of dead negroes, cows and chicken coops.

Thus, objecting to references to the concentration camp as 'an image of an absolute condition', Williams points out that 'while men created the camps, other men died, at conscious risk, to destroy them'.

While some men imprisoned, other men liberated. There is no evil which men have created, of this or any other kind, which other men have not struggled to end. To take one part of this action, and call it absolute or transcendent, is in its turn a suppression of other facts of human life on so vast a scale that its indifference can only be explained by its role in an ideology.

The appropriation of evil to the theory of tragedy is then especially significant. What tragedy shows us, it is argued, is the fact of evil as inescapable and irreparable. Mere optimists and humanists deny the fact of transcendent evil, and so are incapable of tragic experience. Tragedy is then a salutary reminder, indeed a theory, against the illusions of humanism (p. 59).

Redemption and Tragic Transcendence

The assumption, here, is that to speak of an evil as *absolute* or *transcendent*, or to conceive of tragedy as dealing with irreparable facts, is necessarily to regard these evils as *inescapable*—and 'inescapable'not only as past or present *facts*, but, equally, as patterns of the speculative future. Though this assumption is neither semantically nor existentially valid, it is easy to see how it comes to be made. On the verbal plane, *absolute, transcendent, irreparable*, and *inescapable* are all highly ambiguous terms (the first two all the more tricky for having rival technical meanings), and only constant contextual definition can discipline and control them. And, as intellectual forces in our culture, these—and related—terms have certainly helped to sustain a disabling metaphysical social pessimism—the tragic 'ideology' Williams wishes to challenge. (Even the *Four Quartets* are tainted by this ideology, and it is vital to locate, and make critical provision for, these taints.) Unfortunately, Williams's response is not to reassert, and redefine, the necessary distinction between a qualitative description of tragic facts and a prospective tragic determinism but to take over these confusions, unredeemed, into his own argument; and hence, apparently, to disown tragic absolutes in toto.[1]

---

[1] Significantly, the challenge of Camus—just as it exacts a momentary acknowledgment of 'the permanent contradictions of life'—leads Williams, at last, to a momentary emphasis upon this distinction. I have already noted [p. 214 above] the passage commenting on *Le Malentendu*:

> The voice speaks of pity and kindness, but the action speaks of fate, an indifferent, arbitrary and tragic fate. And we have to ask (Camus would have insisted on asking) what are the sources of this perceived condition, especially when it is asserted as

To say that the concentration camp manifests an 'absolute', or 'transcendent', or 'irreparable', condition is not *necessarily* to say that it manifests a pattern 'inescapable' in the future—any more than to say that the evil of *Macbeth* is manifestly 'transcendent' assumes that there can be no redemption in its world. On the contrary, neither the scope nor the depth of 'redemptive' action can be justly perceived without a prior appreciation of the senses in which 'this super-natural soliciting' transcends any 'natural' alienation from humankindness, and in which 'absolute' and 'irreparable' violations of existence occur—both in the world of *Macbeth* and in the world of Belsen, Hiroshima, *apartheid*—or the Moors murders. There are patterns of tragic experience which enact 'the permanent contradictions of life'; and others whose absoluteness is simply an infinite depth in particular viola-

> common. There is an ambiguity, an honest ambiguity, at the centre of Camus's work, for he recognises the sources of this condition in particular circumstances, and yet also asserts that it is absolute (p. 179).

But, within a page or two, this use of *absolute*, in tacit association with a 'common' condition, is suddenly sharply distinguished from it:

> We have to ask, of so honest a writer, the most difficult question. For any man, his own particular condition is absolute. To argue otherwise is to reject actual men. Yet the assertion of an absolute condition as *common* is something else again. We have to ask how much rhetoric, how much lying rhetoric, is involved in that almost unnoticeable transition, under the power of art, from absolute to common (p. 181; original italics).

We, in turn, have to ask of so honest a critic how—quite apart from 'the permanent contradictions of life'—such 'particular...absolute' conditions relate to 'so absolute a conception' (p. 76) as 'the total redemption of humanity'—without rejecting 'actual men'.

tions of being. We cannot always be sure into which of these categories a particular tragic condition falls (the assumption that we can is the tragic illusion uniting total secular hopes with total secular disillusion). But both kinds of tragic pattern are rightly described as 'absolute', both include elements of the 'irreparable'; and both point—twice over—beyond time: in sheer, definitive plenitude of violation, and in that kind of nostalgia for redemption which starts from the recognition that

Time the destroyer is time the preserver,
Like the river with its cargo of dead negroes, cows and chicken
    coops,
The bitter apple, and the bite in the apple.

Tragedy occurs at 'the point of intersection of the timeless with time'. And, while history may be seen either as fixed in changes that do not effect any pertinent change, or as flowing towards a truly healing fruition, we cannot, without rejecting actual men, deny that history carries what it outgrows—that, in this sense, at any rate,

    time is no healer: the patient is no longer here.

No conception of human redemption divorced from this recognition—from the absolute pertinence of the present and past—is finally worthy of humankindness.

Self-redemption even from death?

The ultimate epiphany of absolute violation is of course death. Every truly tragic fact of life has something of death about it; and though the deathliness of violated lives may—in desire for death or suicide—seem to reverse the meanings of living and dying, such totally inverted life-aims merely express death's stranglehold upon such lives.

In death, absolute violation of being is both absolutely inescapable and absolutely incarnate. Death projects 'the permanent contradictions of life' into absolute visibility. Everywhere, around us and within us, this ultimate limit imposes its sovereignty. We live under sentence, not only of our own deaths, but of the deaths of those we live for. Death is the aspect under which nearly all history is present to us; and the future we look towards is already glimpsed as sentenced. These facts of manhood appal us because they are necessary. Here at least 'the mask of Fate' serves recognition rather than evasion. Any 'total redemption of humanity' must either transcend these facts, or be transcended by them.

Williams affirms that even mortality is subject to human self-redemption. For death is not merely 'the bare irreparable fact' (p. 56), but essentially a *response*, to a wider human significance:

Not many works that we call tragedies in fact end with the destruction of the hero. Outside the undeveloped medieval form, most of the examples that we could offer come, significantly, from modern tragedy. Certainly in almost all tragedies the hero is destroyed, but that is not normally the end of the action. Some new distribution of forces, physical or spiritual, normally succeeds the death. In Greek tragedy this is ordinarily a religious affirmation, but in the words or presence of the chorus, which is then the ground of its social continuity. In Elizabethan tragedy it is ordinarily a change of power in the state, with the arrival of a new, uncommitted or restored Prince...

When we now say that the tragic experience is of the irreparable, because the action is followed right through until the hero is dead, we are taking a part for the whole, a hero for the action. We think of tragedy as what happens to the hero, but the ordinary tragic action is what happens through the hero...

What is involved, of course, is not a simple forgetting, or a picking-up for the new day. The life that is continued is informed by the death; has indeed, in a sense, been created by it. But in a culture theoretically limited to individual experience, there is no more to say, when a man has died, but that others will also die. Tragedy can then be generalised not as the response to death but as the bare irreparable fact (pp. 55–6).

Here are the literary roots of Williams's conception of 'the whole action' of tragedy (p. 82), underlying his extra-literary imperatives towards a tragedy of revolution in which 'the whole action we've been living' (*Koba, Modern Tragedy*, p. 242) transcends 'the bare irreparable fact': the 'hero' is transcended by the 'action', the death by the life it 'informs' and even 'creates'. Further, he insists, in ordinary life—even in the most ordinary lives—death can be charged with a variety of meanings; so that it cannot legitimately be tied to modern emphases upon man's tragic aloneness in death:

To say that man dies alone is not to state a fact but to offer an interpretation. For indeed men die in so many ways: in the arms and presence of family and neighbours; in the blindness of pain, or the blankness of sedation; in the violent disintegration of machines and in the calm of sleep (p. 57).

Therefore, to tie death to a single meaning is 'already

rhetorical'; to tie it essentially to loneliness 'is to interpret life as much as death':

Our most common received interpretations of life put the highest value and significance on the individual and his development, but it is indeed inescapable that the individual dies. What is most valuable and what is most irreparable are then set in an inevitable relation and tension. But to generalise this particular contradiction as an absolute fact of human existence is to fix and finally suppress the relation and tension, so that tragedy becomes not an action but a deadlock. And then to claim this deadlock as the whole meaning of tragedy is to project into history a local structure that is both culturally and historically determined.

It is characteristic of such structures that they cannot even recognise as possible any experience beyond their own structural limits; that such varying and possible statements as 'I die but I shall live', 'I die but we shall live', or 'I die but we do not die' beome meaningless, and can even be contemptuously dismissed as evasions. The whole fact of community is reduced to a single recognition, and it is angrily denied that there can be any other. Yet what seems to me most significant about the current isolation of death, is not what it has to say about tragedy or about dying, but what it is saying, through this, about loneliness and the loss of human connection, and about the consequent blindness of human destiny. It is, that is to say, a theoretical formulation of liberal tragedy, rather than any kind of universal principle (pp. 57–8).

Once more we encounter, here, Williams's strategy of reducing *prima facie* tragic universals to totally particular historical peculiarities—and especially to the 'deadlock' of modern 'liberal' tragedy. The first thing, therefore, that needs to be said about this treatment of death is that it involves a crucially one-sided model of tragic tradition. 'Not many' tragedies, outside our own period (and the 'undeveloped medieval form') in fact end, it asserts, with the hero's death. The hero's destruction does not 'normally' end the action; 'normally' there is some sort of reintegration of continuing life; 'the ordinary' tragic action is not merely what happens to the hero but what happens through him. Now perhaps we ought not to look for nice statistics behind such terms as *not many*, *normally*, or *ordinarily*, in this context; but we can hardly avoid asking how, for instance, Euripides's *Medea*, *Hippolytus*, *Hecuba*, *The Trojan Women*, and *The Bacchae* relate to this model; or Senecan revenge tragedy—and its Elizabethan–Jacobean successors, from *The Spanish Tragedy* to Middleton, Tourneur and Webster; or Christopher Marlowe's vision of death—not only the Marlowe of *Dr Faustus*, but the celebrator of *Tamburlaine*, who finally simply acknowledges the bare irreparable fact:

For Tamburlaine, the scourge of God, must die.

Or, a little later, how are tragic destruction and death focused by the poet of *Phèdre*? Certainly, it is useful to stress that tragic tradition cannot be adequately defined in terms of the catastrophic alone; but, outside Aeschylus, Sophocles, and Shakespeare—and the mediaeval Mystery Cycles (an 'undeveloped form')—there is, if anything, greater warrant for a 'normally' merely destructive action than for reintegrating tragic actions. Indeed, not even Shakespeare himself can be wholly claimed for this latter

233

kind of response. *Hamlet*, yes—but *Othello*? *Macbeth*, certainly—but *Timon*? As to *King Lear*, we shall go on disputing its ultimate implications; and meanwhile, on the temporal plane, the new regime at the end seems irreparably weary and sick to death before it begins to begin to take hold of life again. It seems, then, that Williams's assessment of death in tragic tradition again involves a highly questionable (and here wholly unspecific) model of this tradition, to effect his reductive association of 'the bare irreparable fact' with the peculiar sensibility of 'the liberal deadlock'.

There is, however, a notable variation at this stage of the argument concerning tragic tradition: in fact, Williams's treatment of death inverts the tactics already used to query the generality of metaphysical reference within the tradition. To free tragedy for a wholly secular ethos, the argument stresses historical differences within the tradition—implying its compatibility with any metaphysics or none. But to dissociate the fact of death from irreparable destruction, the stress falls upon the 'normality' or 'ordinariness'—the virtual universality outside our modern deadlock—of death as a passing event within a larger continuing life.

And this paradox carries with it two even sharper paradoxes. First, if my evidence holds, it is precisely in respect of metaphysical reference that there is indeed a measure of unity in tragic tradition; while death, there, appears as 'ordinarily' as mere fateful destruction as it is taken up into larger, reintegrating perspectives. Secondly, where tragedy in fact manifests affirmative significances

234

beyond the bare irreparable fact, does this not 'ordinarily' involve a more than secular resolution—as in Aeschylus, Sophocles, Shakespeare, and the Mystery Cycles?

Tragic authenticity

Williams's case could be summed up in the propositions: (*a*) not all traditional tragedy is metaphysical; and (*b*) 'most' traditional tragedies transcend death in continuing life. My own argument reverses these propositions, maintaining that (*a*) traditional tragedy is essentially metaphysical; (*b*) but that these metaphysical meanings are as commonly purely negative—relating to fateful or even demonic destruction—as ultimately redemptive and reconciling. In such perspectives, secular reconstruction alone—even a change of power in the state—cannot suffice to accommodate the poor, bare, forked facts of human death.

Tragic authenticity is largely proportionate to the ruthlessness with which these facts are held before us. To the degree of its authenticity, tragedy cannot allow 'what happens to the hero' to be drained of the facts by 'what happens through the hero'; whatever the ultimate, *cathartic* resonances, tragedy is closer to bleeding to death than to a blood-transfusion. Of course, there are enormous, significant variations in the experience of death, as Williams points out. But even death in 'the blankness of sedation' or 'the calm of sleep', death 'in the arms and presence of family and neighbours', is death. Tragedy as an art projects this fact in its essence, with all the lucidity that sleep or the blankness of sedation may mask. And there is an evident, crucial sense in which death, however assisted by those around, however aware or relieved of awareness, is an action consummated in solitude. (This is why *Everyman*—beyond its doctrinal didacticism—is, clairvoyantly, a tragedy of desertion.) Statements such as 'I die but I shall live', 'I die but we shall live', or 'I die but we do not die', certainly cannot be dismissed out of hand as meaningless or evasive; but nor can they, without evasion, replace a simple, autonomous 'I die'. The first precondition of any authentic tragic redemption is an authentic tragic identity. I am, therefore I die.

This is not a matter of cultural relativities. It cannot be reduced to 'a theoretical formulation of liberal tragedy'. True, we are now conditioned by special communal estrangements, and any increase in real community would significantly modify our tragic consciousness. But not only is it 'inescapable that the individual dies'; it is inescapable that he dies as an individual. And so, too, life itself—the life of the community, here and everywhere, now and to the end of time—is only reaped in personal destinies. Williams himself has often warned us against the vocabulary that can speak comfortably of 'the masses' ('masses' are other people). But by what rationale are we to avoid such habits of sensibility if not by a recognition that the community roots—and re-invests—its own absoluteness precisely in absolute persons? To 'put the highest value and significance on the individual and his development' need not at all imply (though it has often served to imply) a depression of communal significances. On the contrary, there can be no meaningful human community—no properly human values at all—but for communal reverence for absolute personal meanings and claims. *Laissez-faire* atrocities are not the only social atrocities of which we have knowledge. Once we have stepped, not only from 'I die' to 'I die but', but, further, from 'I die but I shall live' to 'I die but we do not die', it may too easily seem only one more step to 'you die but we do not die'—the 'you die' of Stalinist absolutes, Hiroshima relativities, or Final Solutions.

These moral perils—which include liberal perils—are essentially correlative to failures in tragic authenticity. The unfocused ontological gap between 'I die' (or 'you die', or 'they die') and 'but we do not die' may manifest itself simply as confusions in tragic consciousness, or be jumped by tragic moral abominations. What is ultimately at issue, here, is the meaning of sacrificial action.

Starting with our distinction between 'I die' and every kind of 'I die but', we must stress that even 'I die but I shall live' is a genuinely tragic statement—pointing beyond, not away from, the tragic destructiveness of death. It is necessary to stress this because the individual's personal life beyond death is requisite for any true poetic justice, while at the same time both the experienced facts and the redeeming concept of sacrifice require the absolute *reality* of tragic destruction. Sacrifice is sacrificial precisely because it is tragic. Resurrection means resurrection from death. '*Consummatum est*' is not cancelled by eternal significances; the eternal is revealed within tragic consummations. The widespread assumption that Christianity is incompatible with tragedy reduces the Incarnation to

Monophysitism, and alienates Christian humanity from its humanity. Unfortunately, this assumption can draw much support from many Christian cultural actualities, devaluing temporal facts to the point of masking the Christian's own living reality from himself, and defacing his neighbour's incarnate extremities—the reduction of biblical fallenness to habits of high-minded cynicism, and of incarnate neighbourly tragedies to an unearthly Life is a Dream. That the churches have often consented to institutionalized human outrage—and have precipitated nightmares of their own—has not escaped attention. What needs to be more firmly understood is the link between these disfigurements and the failure to take tragedy tragically. A theological culture that fails to keep hold of the absolute human cost of sacrificial absolutes knows 'the price of everything and the value of nothing'. It was the achievement of the Enlightenment, and nineteenth-century liberalism, to re-channel—in the name of humanism—Christianity's arrested responsiveness to bare earthly destruction. It would be a further historical irony if the revolutionary humanism of our time were to loosen its grasp of the bare human pity of such destruction.

How, within secular history, could 'I die' or 'you die' be other than 'irreparable'—whatever the sacrificial fruits for others? Only a personal resurrection could suffice to 'repair' the loss endowing the sacrifice. And even such a transcendent personal rebirth would be redemptive through tragic reality—not from the reality of the tragic. To revolutionary tempers—perhaps naturally sacrificial—this may come home more clearly in relation to others than to themselves. In the anti-tragic culture of *Hamlet*, death (like moral corruption) has been so effectively come to terms with, as a fact of life, that real tragic awareness seems an indecency inseparable from neurotic exaggeration.

> Thou know'st 'tis common; all that live must die,
> Passing through nature to eternity.

Gertrude's jingle exactly ritualizes Denmark's (and even Fortinbras's) domestication of tragedy. Cheer up, that's life—and, after all, there is always life eternal. *Hamlet* is, among other things, a critique of conventional 'maturity':

> Ay, madam, it is common.

And if Hamlet, breaking out from Denmark's standard corruption of tragic consciousness, fails to enact a maturely achieved alternative to its standards, who can afford to whip him for his deserts? The problem of death-as-impinging-on-life is explored further in many other places in the plays and, especially, in the Sonnets. The most definitive confrontation, perhaps, of death as a tragic absolute—or rather, the root of all other confrontations—is Sonnet 64. In the plays, the problem emerges mainly by way of response to actual deaths:

> Never, never, never, never, never.

The Sonnets, however, contemplate death as a tragic threat feeding on life—the fuller the life, the deeper the threat. Most of the Sonnets addressing themselves to this problem unload their tension in subterfuge—though often this is quite conscious, and in this sense less seriously evasive than appears: the appeal to biological offspring, or to the convention of art as a creator of immortality. But Sonnet 64, 'ruminating'

> That Time will come and take my love away

(death is not explicitly mentioned, but this only multiplies the tragic potentialities pressing towards the conclusion) ends with the simple admission of 'ruin' and 'decay'— made irresistibly present through the poem's whole, cosmic build-up—into the presence of present fruition:

> This thought is as a death which cannot choose
> But weep to have, that which it fears to lose.

The intense, dynamic equation in this climax of possession with utter potential dispossession grasps the irreducible sovereignty of human death. No *but* can dislodge this sovereignty. The bare fact that he dies, or will die, may be subject to real pertinent *buts*. But life remains tragically subject to 'he dies' or 'he will die'.

Tragic authenticity and 'total redemption'

Even personal resurrection, then, cannot short-circuit tragedy. Its sacrificial harvest includes the reborn sacrificial seed, but this seed has truly seen death. To die sacrificially, to die for others, is still to suffer absolute destruction. To stand by, in radical proximity, at such a death is to participate in this destruction with an insupportable clarity. Faith in a personal rebirth beyond all destruction does not, unless present facts are evaded, neutralize death. The Christian may, in faith, look forward to a: 'Death, where is your victory? Death, where is your sting?'; but that this faith should have meaning presupposes, and continues to presuppose, the experienced sting of death triumphant. Eschatology is not an alternative to history. 'Death thou shalt die' cannot, authentically, displace 'he dies' or 'he will die'.

Nevertheless, 'I die but I shall live', 'he dies but he will live', are authentic tragic resolutions. They are at once fully tragic and fully redemptive; their tragic triumph redeems, beyond history, the inexpendable spent identity. Only on this condition can tragedy pass authentically beyond tragedy. A deathly abyss separates 'I die but I shall live', 'he dies but he will live', from 'I die but we do not die', 'he dies but we do not die' (unless, of course, this undying *we* were itself read as comprehending the dead—as implying resurrection). Raymond Williams's simple equating of these patterns borrows, for a total, and totally secular, redemption of tragic grief and tragic injustice, the resonances of an essentially transcendent poetic justice.[1] But secular humanism, for all its strengths, simply lacks the resources to repay such a borrowing in hard temporal coinage. No degree of authentic communization of the person can dispose of the person's tragic identity; no community can pass beyond tragedy by by-passing, or forgetting, or dispensing with, tragic

[1] The virtual redemptive equivalence of 'I die but I shall live' and 'I die but we do not die', in Williams's formulation, is reinforced by his transitional pattern: 'I die but we shall live'—which could just as easily be related back to the first pattern (as implying a community of resurrection—the full Christian meaning of redemption) as to the third pattern's committed secularism (though even this *could*, as we have noted, be read so as to imply individual immortality).

identity. Either both tragedy and personal being are ultimately illusory, or 'I die', 'he dies', 'they die', are—whatever the temporal fruits—temporally irreparable. 'I die but we do not die' distils a stoic, heroic humaneness. But as a creed of 'total redemption' it only empties identity of identity.

Even in merely horizontal, historically forward-looking, terms, 'I die but we do not die' lacks the absoluteness to which 'the total redemption of humanity' aspires. Indeed, in the short run, I die but we do not die (assuming our continued coexistence with thermo-nuclear facts). In the somewhat longer run, however, I die and we also die. And if, in the still longer run of historical progress, there is a sense in which we die but 'we' do not die, in the very long run—finally decisive for 'the total redemption of humanity'—'we are' (as Keynes quipped, in a less literal, less intractable context) 'all dead'. This ultimate tragic perspective is sounded with a specially pertinent authority by Teilhard de Chardin:

To ward off the threat of disappearance, incompatible with the mechanism of reflective activity, man tries to bring together in an even vaster and more permanent subject the collective principle of his acquisitions—civilisation, humanity, the spirit of the earth. Associated in these enormous entities, with their incredibly slow rhythm of evolution, he has the impression of having escaped from the destructive action of time.

But by doing this he has only pushed back the problem. For after all, however large the radius traced within time and space, does the circle ever embrace anything but the perishable? So long as our constructions rest with all their weight on the earth, they will vanish with the earth. The radical defect in all forms of belief in progress, as they are expressed in positivist credos, is that they do not definitely eliminate death. What is the use of detecting a focus of any sort in the van of evolution if that focus can and must one day disintegrate? To satisfy the ultimate requirements of our action, Omega must be independent of the collapse of the forces with which evolution is woven.

...If an isolated man can succeed in imagining that it is possible physically, or even morally, for him to contemplate a complete suppression of himself—confronted with a total annihilation (or even simply with an insufficient preservation) destined for the fruit of his evolutionary labour—mankind, in its turn, is beginning to realise once and for all that its only course would be to go on strike. For the effort to push the earth forward is much too heavy, and the task threatens to go on much too long, for us to continue to accept it, unless we are to work in what is incorruptible.[1]

These perspectives extend our consideration of tragic destiny literally to the end of time. But, here, as elsewhere in this whole problem, the most decisive considerations are 'vertical'. And it is remarkable that *Modern Tragedy* repeatedly exposes itself to the force of these considerations, without seeming to register their decisiveness. Thus its finely perceptive pages on *Dr Zhivago* emphasize 'the conception of life as sacrifice, which in the end gives meaning to both the individual and the social histories, and around which, essentially, the novel is built' (p. 167). And there is, here, a full recognition of the essentially religious backbone of this conception—the 'fusion...of

[1] *The Phenomenon of Man*, London, 1959, pp. 296–7 and 335.

the Christian idea of redemption and the Marxist idea of history' (p. 173).

The human crisis of the revolution is that man is born to live, not to prepare for life. The tragedy of Yury and Lara, as of Tanya and of Strelnikov, is a progressive loss of personality, as the destructive force of the revolution extends...

The Revolution, that is to say, is seen as a sacrifice of life for life: not simply the killing, to make way for a new order, but the loss of the reality of life while a new life is being made (p. 171).

These points could not be stated with greater precision. But if 'man is born to live, not to prepare for life', then 'the human crisis of the revolution' is, humanly, irresolvable. 'The reality of life' is expended—really lost—to 'prepare for life'. How, then, in merely secular terms, can 'the conception of life as sacrifice' realize man's vocation 'to live'? How, abstracted from Christian resurrection, can 'a loss of personality, so that the stream may flow again' (p. 171), be other than irreparably tragic—however deep the *catharsis* through the released stream? The impossibility multiplies if we recall the endemically sacrificial, elusive, redemptive vision of 'the long revolution', whose tragic progress we must expect to 'continue as far ahead as we can foresee'. As far ahead as we can foresee, the stream for whose sake the reality of life will continue to be lost will continue to require from men (who are born to live) the loss of the reality of life. Such an 'effort to push the earth forward' is indeed 'much too heavy, and the task threatens to go on much too long'— and much too perishably—for any authentic 'total redemption'. As Williams notes in relation to Chekhov (whose pre-revolutionary perspectives already impinge upon the tragic perspectives of revolution):

What redeems is not the aspiration to the future, but the future itself, and from this they [Chekhov's characters] are cut off (p. 146).

They, too, are 'born to live'; as we, too, and our descendants, are cut off from what we cannot foresee. So, even, is Brecht's secular martyr, Kattrin, in *Mother Courage* (whether we see her simply as a seventeenth-century victim, or as an image of our still emerging community of givers to the future). And it goes for Shen Te, in *The Good Woman of Setzuan*, of whose tragically unavoidable splitting into a saint and a blood-sucker Raymond Williams says:

The only consistent way out is through sacrifice: an acceptance of sacrifice which can become redeeming, as in Christ. Brecht rejected any such acceptance, as he similarly rejected the idea that suffering can ennoble us. Christ, after all, was the son of God as well as the son of Man, and the significance of his action depends ultimately on a superhuman design. *Rejecting the superhuman design, Brecht had the courage to reject sacrifice as a dramatic emotion* (pp. 196–7; italics added).

Raymond Williams also rejects this superhuman design. But does he ultimately reject—indeed, how radically does Brecht himself succeed in rejecting—sacrifice as a dramatic, or anyway as an essential revolutionary, emotion?

There is no way out, there is only an inevitable tragic consciousness, *while desire is seen as essentially individual* (cf. p. 195, above.)

Humanism and Tragic Redemption

A class must be formed which has *radical chains*, a class in civil society which is not a class of civil society, a class which is the dissolution of all classes, a sphere of society which has a universal character because its sufferings are universal (cf. p. 198, above).

And all our experience tells us that this complicated action between real men will continue as far ahead as we can foresee, and that the suffering in this continued struggle will go on being terrible (cf. p. 200, above).

I do not mean that the liberation cancels the terror; I mean only that they are connected, and that this connection is tragic (cf. p. 201 n., above).

...the struggle against suffering learned in suffering... (cf. p. 217, above).

Lawrence misses the decisive question: how can it be that real, potent life is necessarily destroyed by the 'morality...of life itself'? (cf. p. 218, above).

Certainly in almost all tragedies the hero is destroyed, but that is not normally the end of the action (cf. p. 230, above).

...the conception of life as sacrifice, which in the end gives meaning to both the individual and the social histories... (cf. p. 243, above).

I die but we do not die (cf. pp. 232 ff., above).

The crisis of secular humanism and the crisis of Christian humanity remain with us. Their reciprocal questions cannot be avoided. The total redemption of humanity? Yes. Redemption through revolution? Yes. The total redemption of humanity, rejecting sacrifice—or sacrifice (of real men, 'born to live') without a superhuman design? Let any such vision take stock of itself in the mirror of *Modern Tragedy*.

INDEX

247

Index

Index

Index

Index

251

Index

Index